ConnectAbility

ConnectAbility

8 Keys to Building Strong

Partnerships with Your Colleagues

and Your Customers

+ + + + + + + +
+ + + + + + + +

DAVID RYBACK, Ph.D.

WITH JIM CATHCART AND DAVID NOUR

New York Chicago San Francisco Lisbon London Madrid Mexico City
Milan New Delhi San Juan Seoul Singapore Sydney Toronto

The McGraw·Hill Companies

Library of Congress Cataloging-in-Publication Data

Ryback, David.
    Connectability : 8 keys to building strong partnerships with your colleagues and
your customers / by David Ryback ; with Jim Cathcart and David Nour.
        p.   cm.
    Includes bibliographical references and index.
    ISBN 978-0-07-163885-2 (alk. paper)
        1. Strategic alliances (Business).   2. Customer relations.   3. Partnership.
    4. Interpersonal relations.   I. Cathcart, Jim.   II. Nour, David, 1968–
    III. Title.

HD69.S8R93   2010
    650.193—dc22   2009027451

1 2 3 4 5 6 7 8 9 10 11 12 13 14 15 16 17 18 19 20 21   WFR/WFR   0 9

ISBN   978-0-07-163885-2
MHID   0-07-163885-7

McGraw-Hill books are available at special quantity discounts to use as premiums and
sales promotions or for use in corporate training programs. To contact a representative,
please e-mail us at bulksales@mcgraw-hill.com.

Contents

Foreword

IN MY DEALINGS with executives within the auto industry and from various industries over the years, I've never met one who is fully satisfied with the quality of communication among the ranks of leadership. If poor communication exists in management, then it shouldn't be surprising when that lack of quality spills over into the rest of the organization.

A successful business is like a concert orchestra. All the musicians have to be tuned to one another, not only in musical pitch but also in terms of precise timing. That's for starters. Beyond that, excellence depends on the ability of the musicians to be tuned in to the nuances of how the togetherness of pitch and timing is expressed as the music is performed. The greatest orchestras have that togetherness of nuance perfected to the point that all the conductor has to do is keep time and remind the players of what he or she expects by body and facial expression. That synergy helps the conductor bring out the best talent of each individual musician to blend with the union of instruments that make up the orchestra, thereby bringing it to its fullest potential. The result can bring an audience to its feet, applauding with heartfelt passion.

Likewise, in business, the more your team members are in tune with one another—not only in terms of overall mission and united effort but also in terms of the underlying context of how each individual feels fulfilled in sharing the best of his or her potential—the greater the opportunities for success. And the only way to put this togetherness in place for greatest success is through clear communication, at the analytical level and at the more intuitive, emotional level. This means the ability to connect or, as this title has it, ConnectAbility.

As you will soon learn, ConnectAbility is a complex concept, embracing how we present ourselves as we attempt to communicate as clearly as possible as well as how we see others and how they need to be heard, particularly within the context of the business environment in which we happen to find ourselves. So ConnectAbility involves presenting ourselves most effectively, listening so that we're hearing the essence of what's most important, all this in the context of the values of the organization we're striving to make the best it can be. No other concept has ever embraced all three components of excellence in communication.

So what does this mean for you? First of all, it means that you can take control of your situation and decide if you want to be more successful, whether with your colleagues or with your customers or both. Second, it means, should you choose it, that you can learn to enhance the potential for success in your career. You can become a channel for excellence in communication in any circumstances in which you happen to find yourself. As you learn and adopt the principles of ConnectAbility, others will see you as more understanding, less judgmental of them, and wise about the business at hand. You'll begin to sense a power not *over* others, but rather *with* them. As you learn and integrate ConnectAbility into your life, you'll feel more secure in your perspective, since it now embraces that of others within your organization. Others will see you, as you indeed become, more central to what's meant to happen on the road to success.

Third, if you allow the ConnectAbility practice to meld into your personal life, you'll find your relationships, from the most intimate ones to casual friendships, becoming more satisfying and fulfilling. Your family and friends will appreciate being heard more often and being treated in a manner that seems much fairer than what they've experienced in the past.

What's the cost to you? Nothing financial—just the decision to acquire, slowly and surely, the habit of going beyond your former ego boundaries and broadening your scope to include what matters to those you deal with on an everyday basis.

The greatest priority in any business is success, often measured by profit but also by factors such as customer satisfaction. During difficult economic times, survival is a challenge in itself. When losses become too great, the business can no longer survive. Those organizations that do survive do so because they not only can endure the crisis but also are ready to hit the ground running when the market comes back.

Whether a business succeeds or not, particularly in tough economic times, is most often determined by one key factor: communication among employees. Poor communication leads to decisions that don't work. It leads to confusion at points of decision. It leads to errors of fact that result in losses.

In my 16 years at the Mercedes-Benz plant in Alabama and more than 38 years in the auto industry, I've learned the value of involving the entire organization in our operations and the importance of going back to check in at various levels to see how things are going. (At the Mercedes-Benz plant in Alabama, we refer to ourselves as "team members.") Once team members share their ideas, we capture them and integrate the best ones into the organization. Equally important is making sure our team members take ownership for the success of the organization and keeping an open dialogue with them. That's why, we believe, success has always come our way.

People need challenge and you will soon have the ability to demonstrate the promise of persuasive communication and strong partnerships with this new concept of ConnectAbility, as you coach and then applaud others for their successes. As you read, I encourage you to internalize the ideas put forth in this book, to promulgate the values contained in it to make your organization the best it can be.

Bill Taylor
President and CEO
Mercedes-Benz U.S. International

Preface

THERE'S A NEW generation in the workplace—one more focused on process over endgame, on people over paycheck, on personal development over company loyalty. The values of what we might refer to as the "status generation" have yielded to those of the "awareness generation." ConnectAbility fills the needs of this new workplace by providing the skills necessary to work with others—whether as peers or as reports—in a manner that allows for the authentic recognition of others' needs, both social and emotional. Research—under such banners as emotional, social, moral, executive intelligence, and other forms of multiple intelligences—has validated the usefulness of this new approach to interpersonal communication.

Over the years of traveling the world as a teacher, professor, consultant, and speaker, I eventually came to the following conclusion: communication becomes much more effective when defensive ego is put to rest. But putting one's ego to rest is more easily said than done.

I learned from my mentor, the late Dr. Carl Rogers, precisely how powerful communication can become when one's ego is no longer a barrier and openness to another's perspective becomes the focus. Communication is always a challenge. Whether it's management sharing its mission, colleagues working on team projects, salespersons persuading clients, or interdepartmental memos communicating weekly updates, there's always room for improvement. And language has its own limitations. We all have our own personal perspectives, which usually vary significantly from those we're trying to influence. The words we use make all the difference.

Whenever I saw Carl talking to groups, I was amazed by how open he was about his own feelings, in the moment. I invited him to offer the keynote address at a conference I directed, and I was amazed at how fully present the audience became once he took the platform. This was evident every time I saw him speak. When he interacted with small groups, I was equally awed by how others began to open up in a manner that created a kind of electrical charge, so intense was the depth of communication of those who spoke in the group. What did this man have, I wondered, that created openness that was so intensely engaging when he was present and that instantly disappeared once he departed? I was determined to find out.

I pursued a friendship with Carl following that conference, which resulted in his inviting me to meet him and his colleagues in San Diego to head his newly formed consulting unit. Here's what I learned from this experience: The most effective communication occurred when I could, like Carl, put my own needs and concerns aside temporarily and instead focus clearly and intently on what the other person was saying. When this was done effectively, others not only felt heard, opened up, and were much more open to change, but they also felt great about the whole communication process. I was no longer persuading; I was influencing. This could be done not only in private conversations between two people but also in the process of teaching, managing, and more.

Carl and I later collaborated on a paper titled "One Alternative to Nuclear Planetary Suicide." In it we demonstrated how international conflict, reaching back in history, could be resolved when individuals from opposing factions allow themselves to communicate in the manner just described. We revealed how meetings between the Protestants and Catholics in battle-torn Ireland allowed understandings between the two factions for the first time in their history. We revealed how President Carter had used some of the principles of this kind of communication at meetings between enemies. We revealed how Prime Minister Menachem Begin of Israel, President Anwar Sadat of Egypt, and their colleagues met in the United States to bring about the Camp David Peace Accords—the first full peace agreement between these traditional enemies. It became clear to us that this approach to more effective communication proved quite powerful.

But why not apply this principle of communication to business? Why not make management so much more effective, where individuals learned their skills and reached their potential more easily and felt greater motivation? Why not support greater teamwork by teaching this style of communication to team members? Why not increase sales by training the sales staff in the skills of listening and hearing their prospects before delivering the sales pitch? Why not indoctrinate this style into interdepartmental communication to reduce the silo effect? Why not?

And so was born the concept of ConnectAbility, focusing on three aspects of successful business communication: (1) clear awareness of others' perspectives and (2) the ever-so-subtle skill of presenting oneself effectively, (3) within a context of awareness of the desired outcome for any particular business. This book digs deeply into the specifics of what makes ConnectAbility such a powerful concept and shows you, the manager, the professional, the team member, the sales representative, how you can profit greatly from it by learning how to use it in your own sphere of influence.

In the opening chapters, you'll discover the specific components of ConnectAbility as they apply to the world of business. You'll learn that listening doesn't become powerful until the speaker feels heard, and it's the listener's responsibility to ensure this happens. You'll learn that listening is an active process, not a passive one. The loop is closed when acute awareness is combined with professional presentation style within the context of the business. Then you'll see how neuroscience validates these dynamics and just how important the welfare of your brain is to the quality of communication you experience.

ConnectAbility, put simply, is your ability to connect—both in business and in the world at large. Now read on and make it work for you.

David Ryback

ConnectAbility

Introduction

WHAT IS CONNECTABILITY?

THE EXPRESSION OF emotions is subtly controlled in our society. We often aim implicitly to construct our communication to fit in with the expectations of others. What's most important for establishing maximum influence is the skill of knowing oneself along with the group norms for what's considered appropriate by those most highly respected. The greatest communicators really know their audience, and they know how much authentic emotion to display to make the most impact.

One morning, not too long ago, I awoke with a distinct sense of concern. I was aware of my heart beating faster than normal, and I didn't feel my usual self. What was the problem? I had just delivered a highly successful speech at a large corporate meeting. The feedback was excellent. So why was I bothered? I soon realized my concern was a meeting to be held later in the day, about a conflict of power among a number of intense executives in that organization. How would such conflicts be resolved and how did they arise out of a sequence of misunderstandings? Kevin, one of the key stakeholders of my client who had used his strong personality to manage, even cajole, his associates into doing things his way despite their reluctance, had presented an ultimatum: in so many words, it was his way or the highway. I was brought in to facilitate that meeting and bring peace to an otherwise contentious group of individuals. Dealing with Kevin was not a pleasant task; it was like going into a bullfight—people could get hurt if they didn't steer clear of Kevin's anger. And being at the center of that dynamic, I was a prime target if I made the slightest misstep.

1

I therefore made a decision—to start the meeting by declaring my concerns openly, including my own anxiety. "If I tried to convince you that I wasn't at least a bit apprehensive about today's meeting, I'd be lying to you," I began. "So can we put our swords back in their scabbards? And maybe put more energy into listening to one another?" Those opening remarks—made in a confident, assured voice, with a touch of self-deprecating humor—defused some of the tension and laid the groundwork for more honesty and openness. The hurt feelings of those most closely involved in the conflict were more easily expressed, and Kevin took the feedback more gracefully than he might have otherwise.

There was a clear difference between acknowledging my own concerns, that is, sharing self-awareness on the one hand, and the choice to communicate what I felt in a constructive manner on the other. One of the major components of the concept of ConnectAbility is what we refer to as the Performance Factor, which involves (1) the mastery of fear in response to a particular threat through reframing and other skills, and (2) choosing to communicate decisively with a sense of control and intention. The fear is not necessarily denied in the presentation; expressing it allows for a sense of integrity and authenticity, while the message itself is strong and clear. For example, recall Franklin Roosevelt's famous and powerful remark during his first inaugural address, during the Great Depression: "The only thing we have to fear is fear itself."

Communication does not exist without an audience. A speaker speaks to others, aspiring toward a reciprocal experience, whether it be emotional or persuasive, just wanting to be heard and validated or desiring to influence and change the behavior of the listener. What does this new concept of ConnectAbility offer to make that experience in the workplace more powerful, exciting, and successful?

What Does the Concept of ConnectAbility Accomplish?

Given all the models for effective approaches to successful business communication to date, what really holds water? In other words, what's at the basis of the concepts that really work—over time and over the many challenges of communicating effectively with associates, prospects, customers, and so forth? Obviously, many models do have substantial benefit. Otherwise, they wouldn't have lasted as long as they have. But, many have wondered, what is the common theme running through these successful approaches?

The answer is surprisingly simple: an approach to communication that transcends selfish ego and that reaches beyond the person-to-person gap so that both perspectives are respected and understood, ultimately leading to success. To test this statement for yourself, think of the ideas that have captured your imagination, and that you've used—effectively for a while—but that were nevertheless soon taken over by a seemingly more attractive model, promising more benefits.

With that simple answer, however, comes the next challenge: how to acquire the disposition and skills involved in such effective communication so that they're not soon forgotten. How much of that disposition and those skills are an inborn part of our personality, how much is learned in the course of growing up, and how much can be acquired at this point in our careers— whether through reading books, listening to CDs, attending training seminars, or just plain practice? And, finally, how much can we add to our understanding of this by exploring the current research on the neuroscience of business behavior?

The ultimate question becomes, what is the conceptual framework that ties it all together so that we can accelerate our success by more easily coming across not only persuasively, with honesty and integrity, but also with authenticity, *which cannot be faked*?

These are the questions that led to the writing of this book.

Now let's take a closer look at the function of this new and exciting concept. In essence, ConnectAbility is an understanding of the relationship among desired outcomes, roles and expectations, and personal differences while communicating with awareness of the ultimate effect on the listener. It is much more than mere "people skills" and paying attention. It also involves the ability to read the business environment in which the communication is taking place and, of particular interest to those hoping to influence others, presenting ourselves effectively, persuasively, and with concern for the listener—all this in the context of the desired business outcome while maintaining our authenticity. In terms of improving performance, ConnectAbility can be broken down into the following three components:

Awareness Factor

- **Awareness of Influence**—knowing our own emotional disposition and how we affect others
- **Awareness of Others**—reading others well; knowing their needs, concerns, and desires, including the hidden expectations of those who report to us as well as those to whom we report
- **Awareness of Context**—understanding and appreciating the business and interpersonal context in which our communication is taking place

Performance Factor

- **Presentation skills**—expressing a positive energy that motivates others through good as well as bad times
- **Listening skills**—making the best effort to hear and understand others so that the effect of our influence on them brings out the best of their potential
- **Agility skills**—nurturing our passion to get things done, to make the best decision for the moment, even in the absence of all necessary information

Desired Outcome

- **Expectations**—identifying those who are expected to contribute meaningfully to achieve success in our mission
- **Roles**—understanding who the players are in each scenario and who make up the "core group" through which our goals and mission will be achieved
- **Personal differences**—creating a presence that communicates enough caring about each individual to "deliver the goods" with the most positive impact

All this can be accomplished by tuning in very carefully to what's really important in a particular situation. Once we discover that information, through careful listening and research before addressing the situation, the challenge becomes how to deliver our message within that framework while conveying our concern for the welfare of the individual, group, or organization and still being productive. A sales manager, for example, lacking in ConnectAbility, failing at most of the above criteria, will definitely fail to reach potential.

Behind the Concept of ConnectAbility

ConnectAbility is the result of the Awareness Factor and the Performance Factor for a given Desired Outcome, and can be further defined by the formula $CA = (AF \times PF) \div DO$. The ratio of $(AF \times PF)$ to DO illustrates that greater Desired Outcomes require greater effort. Too much energy plowed into an insignificant outcome is a high value of ConnectAbility, but wasted effort. The greater the Desired Outcome, the greater need for higher values of the Awareness and Performance Factors. Small jobs don't require much CA; large, important projects do. When the components—AF and PF—are consistently of high value, great things will be accomplished.

The Awareness Factor consists of reading the underlying relational dispositions (as they relate to the Desired Outcome), both our own as well as those of other people, and reading situations—in other words, Awareness of Influence (AI), Awareness of Others (AO), plus Awareness of Context (AC).

The Performance Factor consists of presentation skills, listening skills, and agility skills. Agility skills measure one's capacity for adapting to ongoing variations in people and changes in circumstances.

All of this is somewhat meaningless until we take into consideration the Desired Outcome. A relationship with no Desired Outcome is not a relationship at all. It is simply a momentary, superficial exchange between or among people. Add a Desired Outcome, such as a business agreement or even a mutual desire for friendship, and suddenly the expectations of and requirements for both parties reach a much higher level.

For example, when two people make eye contact in a hotel lobby (at least in Western cultures), it is natural for them to smile, say hello, or acknowledge each other in some way. That is not necessarily a relationship of great significance. Assuming they ride together on the elevator and exchange comments on the weather, they are still simply in superficial "transaction mode" with each other. But let's assume that they soon discover they're both headed for a boardroom wherein they will be introduced to one another and invited to engage in a discussion of a new business agreement. Then a significant relationship begins to develop.

Once they make this discovery, their dialogue takes on new dimensions. They become significantly more interested in one another. They listen more carefully, interact more intentionally, and take the entire experience more seriously. This is because they are now *invested* in the relationship; if it goes well, they stand to gain something, and if not, they may lose a lot.

The two factors are multiplied rather than added together for one simple reason: if only one factor emerges without the other, then the net result is failure. Much Awareness with poor Performance won't cut it. Neither will great Performance with very little Awareness. Without Awareness of Desired Outcome and overall context, there will be little accuracy in terms of goal setting and accomplishment, no matter how much motivation and energy are put into the endeavor. With great Awareness but poor Performance, goals will not be reached.

In a business scenario, the bottom line revolves around money, and in a social scenario, it revolves around feelings. The more each party is skilled in ConnectAbility, the more likely the relationship will be successful. If they are emotionally aware, meaning they understand the feelings and the factors that affect feelings, then they'll tend to be more sensitive to others and more effective at tact, diplomacy, persuasion, and so forth. If they are context aware, they will understand that the situation is part of the relationship. Dealing with a CEO is not the same as dealing with a receptionist. Dealing with an urgent situation is not the same as dealing with a routine one. And so on.

Assuming a high Awareness Factor, the next category is communication skills. Just being aware is not sufficient; individuals must also be able to *use* this knowledge to achieve an outcome. Communication skills include self-presentation, the ability to express one's ideas effectively, influenced by listening to—and *hearing*—responses, plus agility skills. Agility skills involve the combination of knowing how to communicate differently with different people and knowing how to adapt to evolving conditions. Some might be great at getting along with people of all types but unable to cope with change, which means they'll be handicapped in such relationships. Likewise, we can be good at adapting to change but inflexible in dealing with certain people, therefore encountering many obstacles to success.

The good thing is all of these skills can be learned. You can learn to notice more and thereby increase your awareness. You can learn to listen well and communicate clearly, and you can learn how to read people and customize your responses to the way each person would best receive your communication, without losing touch with your authentic self. Also, you can learn to cope with and adapt to change.

The organizing factor here is the Desired Outcome. One simple way to make your relationships more productive today is simply to restate and agree on the Desired Outcome at the beginning of each venture. Try starting with, "To put today's discussion in context, let's review what we're hoping to achieve through our dealings." Then, as the individuals state and clarify their respective hopes and goals, they'll clarify the focus and eliminate much of the irrelevant discussion.

Awareness and Performance in ConnectAbility

Now let's review the primary components of ConnectAbility—the Awareness and Performance Factors—in greater detail. Can these two factors and the concept of ConnectAbility be clarified and spelled out in a way that makes them easier to comprehend and apply in all business settings? Equally important, what is the relationship among these and the ultimate bottom line of business? Here are some answers.

The Awareness Factor involves:

- **Reading people**—recognizing how people process information, develop relationships, and deal with situations; looking beyond the words to face, voice, and demeanor
- **Recognizing relationship patterns**—realizing the patterns of how people typically interact with others, how others judge them over time

- **Seeing the larger truth**—overcoming ego attachment to face the brutal
  reality of whatever is happening without distortion; seeing the big picture, independent of your particular needs
- **Accepting each reality with all its uniqueness**—being open to the
  uniqueness of that reality and working with it; in a word, agility, the key
  to both the Awareness Factor and the Performance Factor

The Awareness Factor means seeing a situation without judging how it
should be according to preconceived notions, and then allowing genuine intuition to emerge. Assuring that those feelings include the welfare of others is an
important component, as well as the courage to communicate such feelings
with authenticity in the moment.

Now what about the ability, or more to the point, the agility, to "roll with
the punches," to be flexible enough to land on your feet, no matter the challenges you're confronting as they change, more quickly than ever, given the
speed of communication in our digital age? That makes great demands on our
performance skills, what we call the Performance Factor.

The Performance Factor involves:

- **Personal flexibility**—adapting to the differences in people and the
  changes in circumstances; accepting any challenging reality rather than
  resisting it
- **Receptivity**—allowing and embracing new priorities that work and
  changes of direction as they emerge
- **Accountability**—taking responsibility to "do the right thing" and to face
  the consequences willingly as new challenges arise

The concept of ConnectAbility can change the world of business so that
success can be expected and measured more quickly. Unlike applications of
emotional and social intelligence to business, the effects of applying ConnectAbility to a particular setting should show results within months. Why?
Because it emphasizes mandating clear, effective communication in all dimensions throughout the organization and ultimately reaching the end point of
the delivery system—not after the studies have been completed and analyzed

(and shelved); not after committees are chosen to discuss, contemplate, analyze, and write up their findings; but as soon as a decision can be reached by the inner circle.

In this age of high-tech communication, we're often challenged by the lack of nonverbal data that accompany more natural forms of communication. For example, one reason some of us occasionally find it difficult to communicate over the Internet is that we rely so heavily on facial and body expressions as well as eye contact that we feel somewhat lost when communicating by e-mail, especially when there's a need for nonverbal cues in the communication. The insertion into e-mails of "emoticons," little cartoon semblances of smiley faces or other facial expressions, is an attempt to compensate for this lack of eye contact.

We then come to the purpose of videoconferencing, but even that has its limitations. That's why conference calls by phone seem so sterile. Even though some less verbal associates may be saying very little, there's a great deal of comfort just seeing them sitting there attentively, in person. It's also possible they may have something of value to contribute to the conference call but don't feel comfortable interrupting the flow. A particular individual's demeanor and facial expression cue us to invite such valuable contribution, which is otherwise lost in a conference call. It's that aspect of nonverbal communication that makes the relational awareness component of ConnectAbility so important.

Why ConnectAbility Now?

We have to dig deep to nurture those skills that make us more relevant and even indispensable to the organization for which we work. But how do we accomplish this? First, we must pay more attention to the subtext of what's being communicated, to become more aware within the business context, and second, we must build the best of what makes us unique so that we can't easily be replaced. Personal authenticity is a major component.

What the framework of ConnectAbility does, for the first time, is to consolidate all of the elements of multiple intelligences into a business context. It reveals how the basic factors and skills interact and combine in ways that will achieve a desired outcome most effectively.

How to Resolve Conflict and Negotiate Successfully

In any conflict or negotiation, no matter how intense, we can always make sure we understand the other's perspective as clearly as possible. We then make sure to articulate that awareness so the other knows we've made the effort. It doesn't always solve the problem, particularly in the early stages, but it sure beats coming in with fists flying. And sometimes it does wonders.

No matter how adversarial your opponent is, the more you can immerse yourself in his or her culture without losing your own style or authenticity, the greater your chances of succeeding in whatever battle is taking place. Not only will your Awareness Factor be enhanced—you'll understand much more—but so will your Performance Factor—you'll find yourself much more successful in being heard—because you've taken the effort to respect your opponent's framework of values. If you can approach this adversarial situation with a helpful, cooperative stance rather than with defensive aggression, the other party will be much more likely to meet you halfway, with a minimum of exacerbating conflict.

For example, Major General Douglas Michael Stone, appointed commander of high-security prisoners in Iraq in April of 2007, decided to turn around Camp Bucca, a civilian detention center in southern Iraq with 23,000 prisoners. Stone already had experience in successful turnarounds. In the mid-1980s and '90s, he was part of starting or successfully turning around three Silicon Valley high-tech companies. How did he approach his new mission in Iraq? By beginning to learn Arabic and reading some of the Koran every morning, to better understand the culture of the people with whom he had to deal. Within a year, a troubled internment facility went from extremely problematic to the best-run facility in the Iraq war theater. "It was not unlike a turnaround of a nonperforming company," said Stone. He succeeded by becoming more aware of the Iraqi culture, beginning to learn its language and its values, demonstrating the Awareness Factor. One of his strategies was to pay detainees $1.10 an hour if they volunteered in the camp program to learn a new skill. "This is an Arab culture," Stone explained. "It's all about business."

The result? "We've seen an enormous drop in violence," reported overseer Brigadier General Michael Nevin. "Many months have passed without a single incident." Stone believed in battles of the mind, not of killing in the fields. He called things as he saw them, moving right to the solutions that looked promising without worrying about how things might appear to outsiders.

As this story illustrates, by replacing defensiveness with authentic openness and constructive candor, you open the door to much clearer communication. As we'll see later on, appropriate authenticity is woven into the Awareness and Performance Factors, a mind-set that emerges when the two are combined effectively.

The Cutting Edge of Authenticity

Authenticity has been integral to improved communication and leadership in the world of business for the past decade. The path to authenticity is guided by good intentions— truly caring about the welfare of those with whom you work on a daily basis, being aware of their feelings, and communicating your own with honesty and integrity. It's all about relationship—being sensible about the people around you and knowing the feelings that underlie the communications necessary to keep a successful operation flowing smoothly. We call this body of skills ConnectAbility.

The range of benefits of ConnectAbility is broad—from engaging others with authenticity to making rapid business decisions from the gut *and* brain rather than losing opportunities by spending time overanalyzing without using the benefit of fast-acting emotions. Business interactions, whether they be in the areas of management, sales, production, or negotiations—in other words, any person-to-person communication—are best when done with a sense of authenticity. This natural stance says to the associate, customer, even line worker: "I speak from my heart, with passion. What I say is worth your time because I share with you what really matters to me, and it will matter to you too."

How Are You Smart About People?

As Dr. Richard Boyatzis, psychology professor at Case Western Reserve University, and his colleagues have pointed out, leadership in the workplace is ultimately a matter of personal skills that have to do with self-awareness—realizing the difference between your *ideal* self and your *real* self, and then bridging the gap through step-by-step learning.

Here's the basic premise: intelligence takes many forms. We are all familiar with intelligence quotient (IQ), and in recent years, concepts such as emotional intelligence and social intelligence have been popularized by Daniel Goleman, author of the bestselling *Emotional Intelligence*, and Richard Boyatzis, among others. We've stopped asking the increasingly meaningless question, "How smart are you?" and have begun to ask, "How are you smart?" There are multiple "smarts" as Howard Gardner, Robert Sternberg, and Thomas Armstrong have shown us in their books *Frames of Mind, The Triarchic Mind*, and *Seven Kinds of Smart*, respectively, and subsequent works. We now accept such concepts as intellectual bandwidth, intrapersonal intelligence, interpersonal intelligence, moral intelligence, and more.

We've found in our work that there is also such a concept as ConnectAbility. This is the capacity for understanding the context of a multitude of human relationships and for operating authentically within that complex challenge. Those with ConnectAbility enjoy much greater success in all types of dealings because they see beyond the momentary human interactions to the desired business outcomes. This involves understanding human interaction within the context of continuing communication and commerce. It means seeing relationships as essential components of the business dynamic, each unique in its needs and contributions.

The business community has come to embrace this concept more and more each year. One tool that has helped in this respect is customer relationship management (CRM) software. CRM systems have become so commonplace that an entire subculture has grown up around them. International conventions now exist strictly for the exploration of concepts and practices that establish, expand, and sustain relationships over time.

What used to be simply a Rolodex of information, or a database, has now become a complex system among systems for keeping people connected, for example, Facebook, LinkedIn, Twitter, and many others. We've advanced into the understanding and anticipation of people's needs and interests to such an extent that it has taken on the trappings of a science in today's world of business.

What's Ahead?

In the following pages of this book, we'll learn all about the mind, emotional awareness, and how they affect our success at work, helping us to keep our jobs and build stronger partnerships at work. From reading the boss's hidden anger to understanding the facial expressions of workmates, relational communication in various contexts is highly complex and usually unconscious, but a higher awareness of it helps improve business relations.

We'll explore how men and women learn to fake their emotions yet end up with mutual understanding if they just open up to the benefits of ConnectAbility. We'll see how one of the most powerful political figures of his day was a more effective leader because of his ConnectAbility. Both male and female leaders are stronger when they include the other gender's qualities—male practicality and female intuition. How does ConnectAbility originate and develop? It's a complex process beginning in the early years.

"If you can keep your head," as Rudyard Kipling put it, "when all about you are losing theirs and blaming it on you," then "yours is the world and everything that's in it." Reframing negative events into more bearable, positive ones can help. Emotions sometimes rule, but reframing allows us to broaden and build. Negative or upsetting emotions can be signposts to help guide us to our next move, if we handle them with awareness and agility. Look at the context and explore the best strategies for creating win-win situations with the agility skills of ConnectAbility. Resolute awareness conquers fear.

What about optimism and pessimism? According to the theory of learned optimism, perceived self-efficacy—self-confidence based on experience—can be attained by building success one small step at a time, as well as having a good mentor for handling the Performance Factor. In the final chapter of this book, we'll discover that optimism is also based on the meaning of relationships. Otherwise, we're left with learned helplessness.

Success and fulfillment come from finding the "flow" of your work, having a best friend in the office, and connecting with others. If you're the boss, being in touch with your staff members' concerns, authentically felt, will make your team more successful. Otherwise, success means finding the resources available for support. Ultimately, it means basic understanding of and concern for others. In other words, show me the people, not the money.

Negative experiences that damage our self-concept can slow the process of awareness. In turn, that can make us defensive and block our awareness entirely. But those who are more open and less defensive will succeed; they're flexible enough to "slide" into those opportunities that come along and fit their particular skills. "Luck" is just another word for no ego left to lose. ConnectAbility means seeing the reality of business without distortion by the ego.

Finally, what part does money, in terms of wages earned, play in the complexity of meaning and fulfillment? If you haven't yet heard, not as much as we thought. More important are the factors we've been discussing: personal relationships, the meaning of one's efforts in the bigger picture, and authentically being of service to others.

No matter how much you make, there's always someone to compare yourself to who's doing somewhat better. "Reference anxiety" is how psychologists refer to the fact that you're always prone to comparing yourself to those around you—the old "keeping up with the Joneses." And it's so easy to see richer people around you—just turn on your TV. We sometimes ignore those suffering from poverty while we busy ourselves with comparisons to Donald Trump or Oprah Winfrey or whoever is gracing our televisions on a particular evening. But meaning and fulfillment have less to do with money, and a lot more to do with how we use our time with others.

At the end of the day, enjoying productive relationships is good not only for the bottom line of success but for our mental attitude as well. According to an analysis of 1,130 Australians over an eight-year period, those who enjoy their jobs become more extroverted and less neurotic over time. And, according to a recent study, those executives who possessed higher levels of self-regard and other aspects of the Awareness Factor are more likely to yield higher profits in their organizations. If the science of ConnectAbility can head us in that direction, then we're on our way to transforming our careers and accelerating our success with a good measure of happiness to boot.[1]

So what are the specific uses of ConnectAbility? What are its new applications to business relationships? Throughout this book, we'll take a look at the application of this new concept and explain how it can be used for superior performance and more fulfillment at work. From the research on multiple intelligences to applications using the Awareness and Performance Factors in the workplace, ConnectAbility consolidates all this information to enhance success in all aspects of life at work.

CHAPTER 1

Show Me the People

KEY 1: SHARE YOUR POWER
WITH OTHERS

There's a human trait that fears the yielding of power. The delusion is that if an individual were to yield whatever power he or she now has, that person will lose it and all the benefits that accompany it. The truth is, if the individual is secure enough in his or her power to share it with others, that power is enhanced (many times over) through the respect others gain for you when they see your inner confidence.

IN DEVELOPING STRONG partnerships with your colleagues and customers, allow yourself to feel secure enough in your own power as an individual to share it with others who contribute in a meaningful fashion. As a result, you'll significantly enhance your power through the respect others gain for you after witnessing such inner confidence.

If you feel somewhat overwhelmed by these issues, you're not alone. Power over others is a daunting proposition. Sure, there's a primal sense of power that feels good when we can tell others what to do and they are forced, more or less, to obey our commands. It's as if we are stronger, better, more privileged, and more worthy of reward. It's not easy to give up that primal feeling.

But there's a feeling that's more fulfilling in the long run: cooperating with others freely. It's the option to be more productive and successful in the business world because we're part of a team that functions more efficiently and effectively, while making us feel more involved and appreciated on the basis of who we are in terms of our skills and deeper values. We get the job done with less effort and less stress, and in the process, we help others become even more capable of producing their own results.

As Warren Bennis, guru on business leadership and professor of business administration at the University of Southern California, puts it in a *Time* magazine article, "There's a point at which you find an interesting kind of nerve circuitry between optimism and hubris. It becomes an arrogance of conceit, an inability to live without power."

In addition, the Awareness Factor is not the dominant culture in much of today's business world. Rather, the Status Factor—based on competition and conflict, even within an organization—still reigns supreme among many who believe in divided interests rather than cooperation. "It has become clear that nature is filled with competition and conflicts of interest," writes journalist D. Brooks in *The Atlanta Journal-Constitution*. "Status contests came before humanity, and are embedded deep in human relations. We strive for dominance and undermine radical egalitarian dreams. We're tribal and divide the world into in-groups and out-groups."

It's much easier to be simplistic, self-serving, and single-minded in the world of business—easier but not more profitable, at least not in the long run. What really works—in terms of effective leadership, employee loyalty, a more successful marketing approach, superior customer service—is the framework of ConnectAbility. But since confronting the status quo presents a greater challenge, the Status Factor rules the day in more cases than not. This leaves a tremendous margin for success for those who choose the Awareness Factor.

The Status Factor is the favored structure of traditional business organizations, in which power is tightly controlled from top down, resulting in what one expert calls "industry dissonance." More dynamic business organizations integrate ConnectAbility into their value structure. In the following sections, we'll see how the manufacturers at Ford and Mercedes moved toward more ConnectAbility values.

Use all of your strength. When you seek to retain and protect status by using your power over others, you actually diminish your strength. But when you share your power by helping others expand their awareness and learn what you know, you then add their strength to your own, producing even greater capacity for everyone.

Now that we have a meaningful understanding of the Awareness and Performance Factors, we're ready to explore the basis on which the structure of ConnectAbility stands.

- **Relationships are assets.** In any business setting, relationships are assets. As such, they can be created, managed, nurtured, measured, and even discontinued, intentionally and consciously.
- **It's all about who cares.** Business cannot exist in the absence of people relationships. The stronger the relationships, the more potential for success in the business. It's not whom you know that counts; rather, it's who cares whether or not you know them. The more they authentically care— whether the "they" are associates, prospects, customers, or vendors—the greater the potential for success.
- **People relationships make up the business.** When the purpose of a relationship changes, the expectations and "rules" that apply also change. In that sense, the purpose defines the nature of the relationship, which survives until the purpose or Desired Outcome is met. Then that particular relationship ends, or transforms into a new one if a new purpose is agreed on. Therefore, Desired Outcome is the organizing factor in business relationships. Without it, there is no meaning to the relationships.
- **The Desired Outcome defines the business.** All relationships can be evaluated with regard to the Desired Outcome, which may be as simple as casual friendship or as complex as the organization of a federal institution. A marriage contract is one that overlaps broadly between personal and legal aspects of a relationship. The success of a business relationship

always refers back to the Desired Outcome, which might change over time, requiring ongoing evaluation.

- **The key to success is the core group.** Any business, other than "mom-and-pop" operations, is run by a select few, which we refer to as the "core group." Core groups, committed to reaching the Desired Outcome, are the key to success. The ConnectAbility of the core group is of utmost importance, for without an effective inner circle, the business will fail. The potential for success of any business can accurately be predicted on the basis of the ConnectAbility of its core group.
- **Show me the people.** A primary contribution to the structure of ConnectAbility is that businesses are not the brick-and-mortar buildings that house them, but rather the relationships that constitute the social network of the individuals making up the organization. Accordingly, the business is the dynamic interaction between and among its members as they focus on the Desired Outcome. All the rest, including brick-and-mortar physical space, the paperwork files, and the related inventory (if there is such), are merely the physical manifestation of the business, not its essence.
- **We have met the business, and it is us.** It then follows that the business exists whenever and wherever two or more people communicate to achieve the Desired Outcome, including virtual connection over the Internet. A "virtual" business may have no brick-and-mortar home yet be highly successful. But it *must* have a relationship network of individuals focusing on a Desired Outcome.
- **ConnectAbility works at work.** Since relationships make up the essence of any business, ConnectAbility is key to potential for success. Fortunately, ConnectAbility is learnable, through a commitment to education and training. The large body of research on emotional and social intelligences, as well as other aspects of multiple intelligences as revealed by Howard Gardner's seminal work, proves this beyond a doubt.

We improve our chances of success if we appropriately combine the emotional parts of our brain with the thinking component. For example, we pride

> **Hang up your ego long enough to listen.** Yielding to another's version of the truth is not always easy, especially if we're wedded to our own version. What it takes is the realization that such yielding is temporary, just long enough for us to truly understand the other point of view.

ourselves on being in control of our lives. Yet if we get too controlling and analytical about everyday decisions, we become stymied, even neurotic, in our "paralysis of analysis." That's because overanalyzing may interfere with our ability to make quick, intuitive business decisions.

Why are some people of comparable circumstances able to profit from personal investment opportunities while others aren't? When a friend, Richard, first began to invest in real estate some years ago, he found that some individuals, as intelligent as they were in other areas, seemed unable to buy any properties, though they had the financial capability and the desire. What was happening was that they'd analyze all the numbers, over and over, and while that was going on, some much less analytical person, probably less intelligent in the conventional sense but more confident about the big picture and with more ConnectAbility, would move ahead and snap up the good buys. The others, with their overly analytic thinking, couldn't follow through and commit quickly enough. So whether it's communicating with authenticity or making rapid decisions based on both gut *and* brain, ConnectAbility has lots to offer.

The Sounds of Business: Nuances in Feelings

Business is made up of interpersonal communication, whether in person, by phone, over the Internet, or via whatever new electronic instrument that outperforms yesterday's darling device. The most revealing communication, because it reveals so much more in terms of nonverbal information, takes place in person.

Everyone can benefit from the nonverbal aspects of person-to-person communication. Leaders benefit by knowing how their staff members are feeling about the process of reaching set goals. Salespeople benefit by knowing if they're on the right track in terms of sensing the feelings of the prospective customer as they ask for commitment. Team leaders benefit by sensing how close the group members feel to one another as they merge their efforts in accomplishing the most recent mission or project.

We are interested in hearing—and seeing—how others talk, for the most part, so we can sense the subtext behind the context of the situation, making the business venture, whatever it is, a successful one.

Having good sense about people is essential, both within the organization as well as between the organization and its clients or customers. To the extent that a sense of alliance in the first case and a sense of allegiance in the second can be created, success will be enhanced markedly. This accounts for at least a third of the success in both cases. How well we recognize the emotional dynamics underlying business (the Awareness Factor) and how well we perform with the use of this information (the Performance Factor) determines our degree of success.

Where did it all begin? In the next section, we'll look at what came together to set the scene for ConnectAbility, a concept that ties together the tested and proven principles of enhanced communication to make them work in the challenging context of business.

Tips for Advancing Your ConnectAbility

- **Don't overanalyze!** Make important decisions based on both rational facts as well as the gut feeling you have about the deal.
- **When you treat people with integrity, authenticity, and concern, you become more powerful.** This is true both in terms of being effectively persuasive as well as in bottom-line dollars.
- **Listen, show that you've heard—then sell!** Remember: people don't buy until they feel they've been heard.

Where It All Began

"What the heck is going on? Who's that laughing out there?"

A sudden burst of laughter shot through the hallway, making its way through Erik's door and landing on his desk, or so it felt to him, right on top of the numbers he was looking at—to determine whether or not his figures were working out. In charge of sales for his group at a biotech corporation in Atlanta, Georgia, Erik was determined to get the numbers he needed by forcing his sales group to get to their prospects and find out what the sales potential of each client was.

"Is that you, Elizabeth?"

Elizabeth, who had recently moved down from Connecticut, was learning quickly that barging in just to "get numbers" from her new prospects was not acceptable in this work environment. She had encountered a company whose president knew all sorts of important people in the area and they represented a prize potential if only she could "schmooze" him up a bit before demanding figures.

Erik, who had been brought up and trained in Frankfurt, Germany, was more comfortable with a facts-and-figures approach. As in many organizations we know, achieving sales manager status is based more on productivity than on people skills. Erik was mired in the details of getting things accomplished. He demanded to know exactly what percentage of each type of DNA sequencing was taking place at each prospect, how many plates were being processed each week. Elizabeth knew from her clients how hard this was to determine on a weekly basis. So there was tension building between the two. When the laughter, which Erik recognized as coming from Elizabeth, "landed" on his desk, he became furious.

He fired up his computer and distributed a memo, office-wide, over e-mail: "There will be no more laughter in the hallway. This team has got to produce more specific, accurate, and dependable numbers for us to work on. I will not tolerate wasting time, telling jokes, and laughing when we need everyone to focus on the details that are important. Please note this memo applies to everyone."

From that moment on, there was no laughter in the hallways. Nor was there the same degree of productivity that had existed before. Two key players—the best of the group—were preparing to leave, as the gossip mill revealed they were looking for other positions. Tension filled the air, and people left the moment the clock registered 5 P.M. After a few weeks of this, Erik called on me to help him figure out what was going on.

"What were you thinking?" I asked, waving a printout of the memo in his face.

"I just wanted to let them know how serious I was about getting the numbers we needed," he replied, a sheepish half-smile crossing his face. "I thought it was a good move to motivate my people, to raise their morale."

"Erik," I began, "do you realize how people felt when they read this? Do you realize how people react when they're told, commanded, how to think, feel, act? This is modern America, not the old days of bosses telling everybody what to do. You can't just 'legislate' how people will feel, whether or not they can laugh."

"OK," he confessed, "I screwed up. That's why you're here. So what can you do to help?"

I spent the next 45 minutes explaining why this message was the ultimate demotivator. Then I spent the next few days defusing the highly volatile, negative conversations that continued to erupt throughout the building as a direct result of the e-mail. The company had experienced a downturn and had recently been "right-sized," and employees were still reeling from the layoffs. How could someone as smart as Erik make such a blunder?

Everyone reading the e-mail knew that three or four individuals, who were part of a well-known group of yes-men, came in early each morning to talk about others in Erik's office. They were also facts-and-figures people who disliked the informality of the rest of the group. They supported the e-mail, which was seen as an insult and fuel for dissent among the others.

What I couldn't fathom was how Erik could actually believe that his e-mail would raise morale and motivate employees to work harder and longer hours. The term *ConnectAbility* was not known yet in this organization, and this was a clear example of the absence of business intelligence in the workplace—on a grand scale.

As we're learning, ConnectAbility has a lot to do with understanding the social environment, a skill that Erik lacked. I had to explain to him how using e-mail to communicate such a thoughtless memo was wrong in so many respects. Had he dealt with this issue on a one-on-one basis, with a more realistic and personal approach, the results would have been quite different.

The whole point of ConnectAbility is enhanced communication for greater success, whether it refers to the evolution of organizational values, effectiveness of delivery systems, or ultimate sales figures. Communication that is clear, specific, and relevant trumps superficial image and the appearance of smooth sailing at all costs. Ongoing, honest discussion of all relevant factors is crucial.

Certainly there is nothing new since the advent of relationship selling and other aspects of communication involving sensitivity to the other's point of view. But ConnectAbility makes this the highest priority rather than a casual opportunity. Customer service has certainly been headed in that direction for some time now. And for good reason—it works! So by giving it a proper name and highlighting its components, we approach success much more quickly. We create more meaningful teams with ConnectAbility, not only within the organization but also with our clients and customers.

Beginnings

Let's take a look at the origins of ConnectAbility from the research structure of emotional and social intelligence and how it leads us to the importance of emotional awareness (for which we coin the term *Awareness Factor*), along with the need for communicating effectively. Then we'll explore how this Awareness Factor trumps the Status Factor in organizations that exemplify how ConnectAbility leads the way to greater business success.

Since the beginning of recorded history, there has been an ongoing debate about the nature of intellect and emotions and their respective benefits. Typically, intellect was seen as the superior faculty, whereas emotions were seen as distractions.

In the field of psychology, intellect was king over its "peasant" cousin, emotions. One text of the 1930s—*Motivation of Behavior*—characterized emotions as a "complete loss of cerebral control" without a "trace of conscious purpose." IQ tests were first used to measure the *absence* of emotions. But by the 1970s, emotions were finally recognized as part of the intelligence package, thanks in part to the book *Frames of Mind*, by Howard Gardner, wherein he formulated the concept of multiple intelligences, including intrapersonal intelligence (emotional self-awareness) and interpersonal intelligence (social skills).

Finally, the path was cleared for the concept of emotional intelligence, made up of four basic components: emotional self-awareness, self-control over extreme emotion, empathy, and the social wherewithal to integrate these skills. Eventually, intellect and emotion, instead of being on opposite sides of the ledger, became unified in a framework that found wide acceptance not only in psychology but in the worlds of education and business as well.

One reason for the broad acceptance and, in some circles, excitement about this new framework was that it promised and appeared to deliver a highly effective form of communication that could enhance leadership and management to affect the bottom line. The realm of emotions now had validity in doing better at work as well as at home.

Sure enough, psychologists such as Carl Rogers and Abraham Maslow had been touting the benefits of emotional awareness for decades, but these sentiments had very limited appeal to the broader working population. Only when Daniel Goleman's bestselling books *Emotional Intelligence* and *Working with Emotional Intelligence* and its applications to the workplace came to the attention of the marketplace did the media start paying attention. Every magazine had to have at least one article on the topic, even making the cover of *Time* magazine in October 1995. Finally, it was agreed that emotional and social awareness could enhance communication rather than block it.

What can be expected when you make good use of ConnectAbility? What are its bottom-line benefits? What are the dynamics of ConnectAbility within the core group of a business? We'll answer these questions in the following sections.

Bottom-Line Benefits of ConnectAbility

What's in it for us and our business? In the past decade or two, numerous studies have explored the business benefits of what we refer to as Connect-

Ability. In one study in which the sales force of an Australian pharmaceutical firm, Sanofi-Aventis, was taught the elements of the Awareness Factor, there was an impressive 12 percent increase in sales when compared with those who didn't get the training. Here are more studies that show the importance of this factor for greater success in the workplace:

Increased Sales Figures
- The Hay/McBer group found that insurance sales agents with a higher Awareness Factor sold policies averaging $114,000, compared to average sales of $54,000 for those with a lower Awareness Factor.
- At L'Oreal, those selected on the basis of such awareness sold $91,370 more than their less aware counterparts, resulting in a revenue increase of $2,558,360.
- Partners in a multinational consulting firm who were assessed as high on awareness skills delivered $1.2 million more profit from their accounts than did other partners—a 139 percent incremental gain.[1]

Less Turnover
- Another study reported by Hay/McBer found 63 percent less turnover when new hires were selected on the basis of this dimension.
- Those with a higher Awareness Factor hired at a national furniture retailer had half the dropout rate during their first year.
- In a large beverage firm, turnover rates of division presidents dropped from 50 percent within two years to only 6 percent for a similar time period when hiring selection was made on the basis of emotional competence.

Merit Increases and Job Satisfaction
- In a study of 44 analysts and their clerical employees in the finance department of a Fortune 400 insurance company, those with a greater Awareness Factor received greater merit increases and held higher company rank than their counterparts. They also received better peer and/or supervisor ratings of interpersonal facilitation.
- In a sample of 523 individuals, the skill of "perceiving others' emotions" (a significant component of the Awareness Factor) was uniquely associated with job satisfaction.[2]

Leadership and Management Skills

- When 108 senior leaders and their 325 reports were studied in 64 organizations, research revealed that "emotional expressiveness [a component of the Performance Factor] was strongly related to visionary leadership."
- A study of 135 fully employed business students revealed that leadership development using Awareness and Performance Factors could be taught in an 11-week leadership development program.
- A test measuring emotional awareness was able to distinguish between 51 "high-powered" managers and 51 "regular" ones, the "high-powered" ones having higher scores, of course.

Overall Job Success and Team Performance

- A study predicting salary and perceived job success revealed that "agreeableness"—a consequence of both Awareness of Others and listening skills—was a good predictor of salary and that the ability to adapt quickly to new situations was a good predictor of perceived job success.
- In a study of several hundred managers across 12 organizations, self-awareness was found to be linked to superior performance.
- In the U.S. Air Force, recruiters who received a high assessment on awareness skills were three times as successful as their less aware counterparts. By choosing recruiters based on such skills, the air force was able to save $3 million a year, according to a Government Accounting Office report.
- An analysis of more than 300 top-level executives from 15 global companies revealed that "organizational awareness," akin to what we refer to as Awareness of Context, distinguished star performers from average performers.
- Exploring the relationship between emotional awareness and team performance, 349 military team members were tested for emotional awareness competencies. Results revealed that this Awareness Factor was associated with higher performance for the individuals tested not only for themselves but also for the teams they led. It turns out those leaders with higher emotional awareness influence their teams to enhance their own awareness as a group.[3]

Tips for Advancing Your ConnectAbility

- **Leading people is not about telling them what to do.** Rather, it's about understanding how they fit into the work environment and how they can best be understood within that context.
- **Don't just listen; also hear what is said.** We've all heard of the importance of *listening* to others, but *hearing* is the challenge, closely followed by clearly confirming that we've heard the essence of the other's message.
- **Strive to understand others' points of view.** Achieve better two-way communication by "standing under" the other individual's perspective of any conflict or difference of opinion. It's easy (and less productive) to protect our status and image. It's much more challenging (yet definitely more productive) not to let our status stand in the way.

ConnectAbility Within the Core Group

Within each organization is a core group that is chiefly responsible for the success of that organization. That core group might be a working team, an executive committee, or a board of directors. Or it could be an unofficial grouping of people from all three of these categories, typically consisting of no more than a dozen individuals. In this case, the application of ConnectAbility can be modified to take into account the dynamics of this core group.

ConnectAbility, for the core group, increases to the degree that there is a higher degree of alignment with stated goals as well as with each other. Trust levels must be high and cooperation must be natural and uninhibited. Good dynamics within the inner circle of productivity involve deep person-to-person communication and adaptability to changing circumstances and challenges. The greater the Desired Outcome, the greater the combination making up the level of ConnectAbility.

There is a strong focus on dynamics within the core group, because it is this group of individuals on whom the success of the entire enterprise depends. Without the interpersonal sensitivity and adaptability, this inner circle cannot perform to its highest potential, thereby blocking success no matter how much awareness there is to the individuals outside. Also, no matter how great the Awareness Factor or the effectiveness of the inner circle, unless they are aligned clearly with the goals of the organization (Desired Outcome), then the highest success will not be forthcoming. Finally, the greater the Desired Outcome, the greater the demand on the elements of ConnectAbility.

Malcolm Gladwell, in his book *Blink*, teaches us about how quickly decisions are made by those who are good at what they do, whether experts at art or sports or business. *Thin slicing* is the term he uses to depict how little information such experts use to make their astute decisions. The best of them waste little time thinking about the unnecessary. When they're trucking on all cylinders, their minds are powerhouses of instant decision making—every thought a blink. In his book *Strangers to Ourselves*, Timothy D. Wilson writes of "the adaptive unconscious," which "does an excellent job of sizing up the world . . . setting goals, and initiating action in a sophisticated and efficient manner." At their best, core groups are made up of personalities that complement one another. The best core groups operate on this basis of "blink," complementary personalities, unreserved honesty and clarity in making quick decisions, and in deep commitment to the Desired Outcome.

Where Do You Stand with ConnectAbility?

Here are some key questions to help you discover where you are in the context of ConnectAbility. As you read each question, consider how productive your relationships are within your own job and career and what each question offers you in terms of potential for change. Do you dare take the initiative that might result in changes you only dreamed of? Ponder each item without rushing through it. Give yourself as long as five minutes for each one. Only by carefully considering the intent behind these questions will reading the rest of this book be most meaningful to you.

1. As you consider your own current work environment, how does all that you've read here so far fit your own experience?
2. How can you become more clearly aware of the overarching goals or mission of your organization, so that you become more integrated into that effort?
3. Having considered all this, what can you do to move in the direction that you now choose?

Unfolding Your Agile Self

Do you ever wonder what you really have to offer the workplace? What knowledge, talents, and skills do you possess that could benefit others? You see, others will recognize whatever is placed before them in an inviting proposition. It's usually not that others fail to recognize what you have to offer, it's—you guessed it—yourself! Awareness starts at home, with the best measure of what special contribution you make essentially because of your unique person. Agility is the capacity to be open to changes and to roll with the punches to bring out your best resources to fit the challenge at hand.

"How do I use who I am on earth for a purpose that's bigger than myself?" asked Oprah Winfrey in her *Newsweek* article on leadership for the 21st century. "My answer always comes back to self. There is no moving up and out into the world unless you are fully acquainted with who you are. You cannot move freely, speak freely, act freely, be free unless you are comfortable with yourself." Jack and Suzy Welch, in their opinion column appearing in *BusinessWeek*, made a similar point when they referred to authenticity as "the foremost quality business leaders must possess."

Each of us has more to offer than we realize. Our age, race, gender, and educational achievements do identify us. But with the Awareness Factor, they are less likely to limit us. Given our age, gender, race, and so forth, according to simplistic and outmoded thinking, we *ought* to think in a certain way so as not to upset our place in the status of things; to harbor a certain philosophical approach; to allow others to see our behavior as predictable and easy to manipulate. But becoming more aware of our emotional resources in terms of self-awareness and openness to change (agility), facing the reality of our potential, we can liberate our thinking from this delusion and become much more adaptive to whatever environment we find ourselves in.

The Corporate Shift to ConnectAbility

Laughter and smiles are often signs of relaxed comfort, quite the opposite of hierarchal power imposed on the organizational structure, where scowls are more common than smiles. In such status-based organizations, power is assigned according to rank, and there is little wiggle room for the free expression of inner resources on the part of "lower-ranking" subordinates. Here status reigns supreme, not open awareness.

True power can never be lost, except at the point of a gun, of course. In a free and open culture, an effective leader who yields power with generosity and support will only become a more steadfast and credible leader, resulting in greater loyalty and commitment within the organization. Beyond that, the Awareness Factor approach to leadership and management with Connect-Ability encourages much more creative productivity within the organization. The Status Factor approach, ironically, results in more conflict and sense of frustration throughout the organization, since there is little opportunity to express and resolve such conflict. So the end result is low morale and high turnover, though no one admits to exactly why. The status quo is maintained with flagrant disregard for changing business realities.

Consultants often hop on the bandwagon of their employer's status thinking and neglect to challenge existing ways. They often don't appreciate the need for the Awareness Factor in business—what is going on out there in the

Face the brutal truth. Being righteous is so easy—listening is the challenge! Stay with your deepest awareness of what is real as you gain more information, even if that differs from the flavor of the day.

marketplace, for instance—before leaping into new, reengineered makeovers. In his book *Early Warning*, Ben Gilad refers to this blind delusion as "cocoonism," where there is little awareness of outside factors, allowing the Status Factor to reign supreme from within. From Gilad's point of view, overdependence on those consultants that aren't up to par, sometimes going from one to another, results in a situation where less and less attention is given to hearing the realities of the outside world.

According to Gilad in an explanation of his term *industry dissonance* from *Early Warning*, "Powerful leaders evoke powerful mechanisms to explain away the facts, sustain the denial, and dismiss the signals from the outside world that don't support their views." Once the Status Factor reaches critical mass, often with the help of expensive but ineffective consultants, the Awareness Factor can get overrun. Gilad maintains that "when reality and conviction are at odds with each other, conviction often wins." The hierarchy-driven delusion can lead to "groupthink," creating a blind spot where awareness would otherwise have its rightful place. This is exactly the process that led to energy brokers at Enron, not to mention AIG and other financial institutions, giving in to greed and to the ultimate demise of the organization.

In addition to such victims of "industry dissonance" as the late Enron founder Kenneth Lay and CEO Jeffrey Skilling, there seems to be a movement, perhaps due to the dramatic economic shifts occurring at the start of the century, in which the status-loving, jet-setting, deal-making celebrities of the 1990s are being replaced by awareness-sensitive leaders who are more performance oriented and less egocentric. Some clear examples of this trend are Disney's preference for consensus builder Robert Iger over the more domineering Michael Eisner; Hewlett-Packard's choice of low-key Mark

Stand up for your convictions. Escaping the "cocoon" of status delusion is challenging. It requires that you stand up for your personal convictions, even in the face of "groupthink." It helps to test your ideas out with those who appear sympathetic to your thinking.

Hurd over high-profile Carly Fiorina; and Intel's transition from charismatic, rough-and-tumble Andy Grove to the more diplomatic and soft-spoken Paul Otellini.

When Otellini took over as CEO in May of 2005, he converted Grove's old antagonistic philosophy of "only the paranoid survive" to the more discrete "praise in public, criticize in private." To integrate a sense of Connect-Ability into the company culture, Otellini hired sociologists and ethnographers to better discover what emotional ties potential customers had to certain product images in one particular region over another. Intel even hired doctors to work with their ethnographers to explore which technologies the elderly might find most useful in monitoring their vital signs or tracking how victims of Alzheimer's ate. "I have seen more flexibility," admitted Sony vice president Mike Abary, in a *BusinessWeek* article, "more of an open mind-set than in years past," appreciating the Awareness Factor of Intel's increasingly collaborative attitude.

When Bill Ford Jr. took over as CEO of Ford Motor Co. after firing Jacques Nasser, it became clear that the corporate culture there was shifting away from Nasser's aggressive, hierarchical status style to Bill Ford's more collaborative awareness style. Bill is a passionate environmentalist and student of Buddhist philosophy. He's much more people-oriented than Nasser, who shook up the company with his hyperaggressive management style. Yet Bill Ford is no pushover. As Mark Fields, president of Ford's Americas division, puts it in an issue of *Time* magazine, "You don't have to be a tyrant to be tough."

Though Bill Ford has since yielded the presidency to former Boeing executive Alan Mulally, he maintains a strong influence over his family's company, remaining executive chairman. No lover of hierarchy, he answered in a *Newsweek* article when asked about his giving up his title of CEO, "I've always said that titles are not important to me. . . . What's important is getting this company headed in the right direction."

After handing the CEO mantle over to Mulally, Ford said, "I have a lot of myself invested in this company, but not my ego. I just want the company to do well. It's not about me."

Continuing the priority of ConnectAbility at Ford Motor Co., Mulally was characterized in the *Wall Street Journal* as a new-age Lou Gerstner, a "gregarious man . . . an executive with a strong track record for building team-work in a large organization." This fit with Bill Ford's style of maintaining the ConnectAbility of his management team—"searching for a combination of subordinates who shared his desire for a teamwork-oriented, collegial man-agement culture." In Mulally's own words, as described in another *Wall Street Journal* article, "You talk to customers, dealers, Ford employees, UAW, your suppliers, your investors—everybody. . . . I know that's what I have to do. I need to network with these groups."

While General Motors and Chrysler floundered in 2009, Ford's U.S. market continued to grow. Upon ascending to the leadership of Ford, Mul-lally had acquired what he jokingly termed "the biggest home-equity loan in history"—cash and credit worth almost $30 billion—a brilliant deal, accord-ing to financial analysts. With its focus on smaller cars and electric vehicles, Ford was in much better fiscal shape than its competitors, an indication that ConnectAbility does work where other approaches are not as nimble.[4]

The High Cost of Mercedes Status

Look at what happened when Daimler-Chrysler replaced the tumultuous Jur-gen Schrempp with cost-cutting, production-oriented Dieter Zetsche (or Dr. Z, as he was affectionately referred to in television commercials). This was a clear case of Schrempp's personality-driven leadership style being supported by his supervisory board (the German equivalent of a board of directors) until it became too obvious that his hierarchy-dependent status style was no longer tenable. Though he tried to turn things around to become more hands-on and engineering oriented in early 2005, the supervisory board ultimately turned to the more laid-back, people-oriented Zetsche.

Whether it was the cheap American dollar hurting American sales or poor quality control in new Mercedes output, Schrempp was in water too deep for his board to support him any longer. Even the new, small Smart "city car" sold in Europe was losing money—about $400 million in 2004. It didn't help when Schrempp was taken to court by Las Vegas financier Kirk Kerko-rian after Schrempp told a *Financial Times* reporter in 2000 that he always intended to make Chrysler a division rather than an equal partner. At board meetings, fund managers were breathing down his neck. All this lack of ConnectAbility built up to a critical point. Once Zetsche took over, things began to turn around for the company. After his reign began as CEO, Daimler-Chrysler's stock went from slightly above $50 to over $80.

In 2007, Schrempp's decision to acquire Chrysler was undone when the private-equity firm Cerebrus Capital Management negotiated to purchase a controlling share of Chrysler. However, Cerebrus later purchased 80.1 percent of Chrysler for $7.4 billion. Part of the failure of the original Daimler-Chrysler union was due in large part to Chrysler's continued manufacture of gas-guzzling SUVs and pickups despite the soaring cost of gasoline—hardly an intelligent decision, people-wise or otherwise.

Overall, there appears to be a tide in which ConnectAbility is finding its place. In the next section, we'll see this quite clearly in the management shift at Home Depot.

Transition to ConnectAbility

"NARDELLI OUT" shouted the headline of the *Atlanta Journal-Constitution* in the first week of 2007, with the subhead explaining "Embattled Home Depot CEO's Abrupt Resignation Pleases Investors, Though His Exit Will Be Expensive." Despite his $154.3 million compensation in just one year—2005 —Nardelli's by-the-numbers approach "alienated longtime employees and some shareholders with what many perceived as an autocratic style," according to the article. Clearly, this was an individual with a hierarchy-based status approach to business—an "organization guy," according to Home Depot cofounder Bernie Marcus.

So whither the fate of Home Depot from this point? Toward ConnectAbility, of course. Nardelli's successor was Frank Blake, introduced by the same newspaper with the headline "New CEO Brings New Tone." Replacing what the paper characterized as Nardelli's "tone deaf" approach, Blake was characterized as "getting along with people, according to people who know him."

But, with so little known about this new figure in leadership, how can we be so sure that Blake can be characterized as an awareness-type leader? Listen to what others have to say.

Former GE chief Jack Welch, for whom Blake had worked, had this to say about him: "He has very deft political skills. . . . His intellect always won the day over shouting." Former Home Depot chairman Bernie Marcus called him "a great listener and a good people person." Ben Heineman, GE's former general counsel, judged Blake as "courtly," with a deft "public touch." "He will listen twice as much as he speaks," said the chief of Southern Company in Atlanta. "He doesn't need to hear himself talk, but when he does talk, you will want to hear what he has to say because it will be very thoughtful and very credible."

Blake himself told the media: "You'll see the associates and customers at the top, and me as CEO at the bottom." After meeting with the new CEO, Home Depot cofounder Arthur Blank reported: "I got a sincere feeling that he wants to marry the best of the past with the future, and that was really refreshing," comparing Blake's awareness-oriented approach to Nardelli's status-oriented "financial metrics" approach. The term *metrics* brought boos from shareholders at the 2008 annual meeting. What they wanted was more "aprons" on the floor, to which Blake promised to "improve the knowledge base at our stores" by hiring more savvy home-building professionals—professional plumbers, electricians, and so on.

When the economy became problematic, what did Blake do? He waived his $1.2 million cash bonus for 2008 and decided that none of the company's top executives would get raises for 2009. All of Home Depot's executives forfeited the use of company cars and gave up their "tax gross up" payments to cover income taxes.[5]

And what happened to Nardelli? Well, he was smart enough to keep open the bridge to his former network at General Electric. Many in this network subsequently had strong ties to Cerebrus, the private-equity firm owning newly separated Chrysler. Like a convoluted, dark opera, Nardelli eventually became the CEO of Chrysler, thanks to the support of his former mentor, Jack Welch. The loop was closed.

The Dirty Little Secret—Lack of Candor

Overall, there seems to be a shift in the corporate mind-set—from status-oriented, hard-driven, personality-cult, top-down leadership to more relationship-oriented, collaborative, communication-based types. According to Judith Glaser, author of *The Leadership DNA*, as quoted by *The Wall Street Journal*, over time, "the 'me-centric' approach can morph into a bullying style and create a vindictive, politicized atmosphere in which subordinates battle each other to win the boss's favor." The hierarchy-based Status Factor with its domineering leaders is giving way to the hierarchy-independent Awareness Factor with consensus building and a priority for grassroots sensibility.

As Jack Welch puts it so eloquently in his book *Winning*, to win at business, "you should listen to smart people from every quarter." In his chapter on candor, he characterizes it as "the biggest dirty little secret in the world"—realizing how rare it is in the corporate culture—"lack of candor permeates almost every aspect of business. . . . When you've got candor," he concludes about this keystone of the Awareness Factor, "everything just operates faster and better."

It all starts at the top, of course. At least it gets its support there. Higher management takes ultimate responsibility, whether it be toward awareness or status in the organization.

In the absence of ConnectAbility, the only apparent release for such frustration may be for those higher on the organizational chart to lord it over those in the lower ranks, creating the delusion that power is the ultimate reward rather than real contribution to the common goal. Such an organization promotes status as the manifestation of power, stifling each level of the hierarchy in turn, from top to bottom. Contribution to the common goal becomes a low priority, since each individual is now busier protecting his or her turf than being meaningfully productive.

With ConnectAbility, generosity of spirit permeates the organization, benefiting even those at the lower levels. The paramount value is contribution to the common goal, superseding rigid demarcation of status. The

Hone the fine skill of your inner honesty. Don't let politeness prevent you from telling your personal truth. Somewhere between the boundaries of politeness and rudeness a calm area of inner truth is revealed, with tact and sensitivity to the outcome. Honesty is a finely honed skill, not a personality trait.

predominant aspect of communication is accessibility and support. Disappointments are dealt with quickly and fully, quashing any sense of unfairness or conspiracy.

The Courage to Communicate with Awareness

The courage that Jack Kennedy displayed in facing down the Cuban missile crisis, that Churchill showed in fostering Britons' courage to show a stiff upper lip in the face of Nazi bombing, that any leader musters when he or she reaches out for the right decision and the rest of the organization subsequently breathes a sigh of relief—this action is brought about by the courage to recognize the prevailing sense of what truly is, beyond ego-bound attempts to confuse the issue.

The word *courage* has its root in the old French word *corage*, associated with the modern French word for heart—*coeur*. Courage is heartfelt. It stems from deep within, from the real self. True leadership is heartfelt; otherwise it is mere management.

The deepest form of leadership is the ability to stand up to the greatest of crises, reach down to one's real self in terms of naked courage, and communicate with heartfelt eloquence a solution that others can understand instantly and embrace collectively as a surrender to what truly is—the skills of ConnectAbility—that erases all the myths, spins, and deceptions that hid the basic truth until that very moment of revelation. But such awareness does not have to be postponed until such crises test the leader; it can exist from day to day if the leader and the organization choose to value it as a working priority.

All humans are complex and so are all leaders. There is no pure essence of awareness that isn't met by complex factors teasing its saintly values. The finest quality of awareness, when it does prevail, is what remains after all human complexities fall away to allow the true self to shine through at critical moments. By reaching down to the real self, a leader can simultaneously reach across to the collective awareness in the audience being addressed. Paradoxically, the uniqueness of the leader becomes integrated at that moment with the essence of uniqueness of the individuals being addressed. It's as if the sense of uniqueness, though real for each individual, is at the same time a myth. In other words, we're not that different from one another in our deepest fears and concerns. The quality of awareness—that all feel through the eloquence of the leader's sharing his or her true self, in that moment—transcends any differences.

Another way of putting it: the most unique and unutterable aloneness we can feel is in itself a universal experience. The greatest leaders have the courage to bridge that universal quality. Remember FDR's historic statement, "The only thing we have to fear is fear itself." With that simple statement, he reached all those who heard his words at the core of their inner being. ConnectAbility, at its essence, is the most powerful stance for mastering emotional communication in any business organization in order to bring out the most productive potential in individuals comprising the workforce. Whether it's laughter in the hallway or tension in the boardroom, ConnectAbility masters troubling emotions and creates an opportunity for greater success at every level of the organization.

In this opening chapter, we've clearly defined and explored new insights into the basics of ConnectAbility. We looked at how the corporate culture is using these new insights to head increasingly toward the values of ConnectAbility.

In the next chapter, we'll look at how our brain functions in the process of attaining ConnectAbility. We'll explore current research in neuroscience to better understand exactly how we process information when communicating with our clients, associates, bosses, and reports. Through the new technology of magnetic resonance imaging (MRI) and positron emission tomography (PET), we'll see exactly how our brains work, for better or worse, in the world of business. Knowing what happens inside our skulls can enlighten us about how we communicate on a daily basis. Mastering the workings of our brains offers insights into greater success in the world of business.

Tips for Advancing Your ConnectAbility

- **Listening is a full-time challenge.** Successful leaders are great listeners, not just to their reports but also to their customers, the competition, and the overall context of marketplace conditions. It's all about the people—those who work for us, those who buy from us, and all those who provide the resources that affect our business.
- **Candor**, according to Jack Welch, is the key ingredient of successful leadership. Authenticity is key to ConnectAbility. Listening and awareness are key to staying on top.
- **Persuade audiences at a deeply passionate level.** When we can get to the core of our own deep concerns, and communicate them eloquently with the awareness of others' concerns, we have the power to persuade others effectively and consistently.

CHAPTER 2

The Neuroscience of ConnectAbility

KEY 2: COMMUNICATE WITH AUTHENTICITY

Neuroscience research reveals that open, authentic communication with your colleagues and customers builds healthier brains, while feelings of frustration and alienation can be harmful. When you opt for flexible and decentralized chains of command with support and openness, you're better able to maximize personal welfare and achieve overall business success, resulting in less conflict and stress, greater trust and support, and an increase in overall output, sales, and profits.

THE LATEST DISCOVERIES in neuroscience reveal that the workplace is a dynamic exchange of brain-to-brain influence. Such influence can be used to enhance the power of an organization if we learn to harness it by understanding how we affect one another, for better or worse. Our purpose in this book is to set the stage for learning how our awareness of the intent and needs of others in the workplace—whether they be our colleagues or customers—can make us and our business more successful over time and make our work much more meaningful.

Each workplace setting is unique and each one changes from week to week, sometimes minute to minute, given global electronic communication. In a highly competitive economy, with globalization resulting in more and more outsourcing and oversupply of labor, the workplace is less inclined to make the human factor a priority.

The more closely we work with someone, the stronger these influences are. It's all about social interactions and how we handle them. It's also about the components of multiple intelligences and how they relate to social awareness and relationship management. ConnectAbility places primary focus on the awareness of external factors in our work environment as well as communication skills—elements of social awareness and relationship management, respectively—rather than self-awareness and self-management. Utilizing these two components together, one will achieve greater success in the business world.

This new paradigm allows a closer look at the emerging findings from the fields of social psychology and neuroscience, and how we influence one another much more than we ever knew. As Daniel Goleman puts it in his book *Social Intelligence*, "Our most potent exchanges occur with those people with whom we spend the greatest amount of time day in and day out, year after year. . . . During these neural linkups, our brains engage in an emotional tango, a dance of feelings . . . sending out cascades of hormones that regulate our biological systems. . . . That link is a double-edged sword . . . as we realize how, through their sum total, we create one another."

This chapter will focus on neuroscience—the data obtained from brain scan technology (PET scans and fMRIs)—that allows us to see into the brain and understand much more scientifically how our brains function as we interact with others. Social neuroscience is emerging as a new way of understanding the dynamics of communication. The business world cannot afford to ignore this new technology if it hopes to fine-tune the skills of influence and persuasion in the workplace.

Use both sides of your brain. Understanding others' perspectives and the influence of your own presentation in business are the two keystones of ConnectAbility. To do both well, use your brain—both the emotional part as well as the thinking part.

Doing Right Is Sometimes Better than Being Right

I couldn't erase from my mind the impact of what I'd just heard. A young woman stood at the dais, her silky hair framing a demure, almost schoolgirl-like smile. Yet she was talking about war, with all its grim and mundane details—how her role in active combat had transformed her naïve, innocent lifestyle, with which she'd begun her experience, into that of a crafty warrior in Iraq. In a talk to promote her book, *Love My Rifle More than You*, Kayla Williams was sharing with an Atlanta audience her experiences as a translation specialist in Iraq.

As she and a platoon of infantrymen traveled through an area in Baghdad called Dura, they came across a Christian monastery and knocked on the door. A robed priest met the soldiers. With quiet dignity, he invited the soldiers to join the other priests in Easter prayer. When he was asked whether there were any weapons, he admitted to having an old rifle—a Kalashnikov, at least 30 years old, with about 20 bullets—used, he said, to ward off looters and other threats to the monastery.

The lieutenant barked orders for it to be confiscated.

The priest begged to be allowed to hold on to the rifle to defend himself and the other priests and to protect the only computer in the entire neighborhood as well as religious relics. The infantry lieutenant decided that, according to his orders to disarm the local organizations, he must take this rifle, though it was clear that it presented no threat but, on the other hand, was the only form of protection for this monastery.

As I sat in the audience, I heard Ms. Williams share her concern for the welfare of the priests, and how crestfallen she became when the officer in charge decided to take the weapon. He was acting according to his orders in a strict literal sense, without regard for Awareness of Context; on a rigid interpretation of his instructions rather than with regard for the reality of what was obvious to any sensible individual. It was crystal clear to Ms. Williams that this rifle was not what was intended in the orders given, yet, following the literal meaning of the instructions, the rifle was taken.

This is an excellent example of what really is going on in terms of human awareness versus what demands to be done in a strict, literal status-oriented context. What the lieutenant should have done, according to his instructions, was to remove all weapons from mosques, schools, and organizations. But, according to Ms. Williams, the orders also stipulated that families could keep one weapon for self-protection—to protect themselves from looting. This lieutenant could have made a personal judgment call on this. He could have interpreted his orders differently if he wanted to, if he really understood the Desired Outcome.

The old rifle was tossed into the back of the truck and the lieutenant didn't look back, ordering his men to climb in. The job was done.

But Williams harbored a sense of what we refer to as the Awareness Factor. She felt that they were abandoning these poor priests to a fate she could not imagine. The word on the street was out: the monastery had been disarmed. She gave them until dusk—maybe the night—before some gang or other would come busting through their door.

Luckily, when Ms. Williams shared her feelings about this incident with a superior officer, who apparently did have the skills of ConnectAbility, that individual took it upon himself to revisit the monastery and gave the priests the rifle they needed so desperately to protect themselves. Though this was against strict military protocol, the officer did the right thing in this situation to produce the Desired Outcome.

Climbing over the back fence, to keep the transaction private, the captain knocked on the door. The same priest answered. Silently and without ceremony the captain hastily handed the AK to the man. And he was gone again, even before the priest could thank the captain for this priceless gift.[1]

Clearly, facing what is real for all involved (Awareness of Context) takes a more thoughtful and heartfelt approach to responsible decision making (Desired Outcome).

Business is essentially about realizing profits and the power to convey to others (Performance Factor) what we know needs to be done (Awareness Factor) in order to achieve success (Desired Outcome). Effective communication is not optional; it's a mandate for success. When done well, it becomes natural and comfortable for both speaker and listener.

Being "right" is not always the goal. Being "right" in the narrow-minded sense is often a perspective that is tainted by our own unique and selfish viewpoint, blocking out what others see and have to say about whatever it is we happen to be focusing on. As the renowned historian Arnold Toynbee put it in his essay *I Agree with a Pagan*, "Trying to do right does mean fighting oneself, because . . . each of us feels and behaves as if he were the center and the purpose of the universe. But I do feel sure that I am *not* that, and that, in behaving as if I were, I am going wrong." We all see the world—what appears "right"—from our own personal center. The Awareness Factor puts that center into more objective focus, closer to that of others, where it is much more likely to be accurate.

The goal of ConnectAbility is communication, with the end point being the success of the business enterprise, but not at the expense of integrity, ethics, and even our deepest sensibilities that transcend being defensively "right." There is something deep within each of our souls that resonates with what is *ultimately* considered right when looked at over the long run from an organizational perspective.

With soul and substance equally important, the neuroscience of ConnectAbility reveals how to capture both in our work. The skill involves using our "brain power" to engage authentic feelings to express them. The rest follows naturally, according to the latest neuroscience research.

It is one thing to talk about how personalities and their thinking affect others. It's another to be able to point to concrete aspects of what happens inside the brains of such individuals as well as to the brains of those they influence. Now we have a technology—neuroscience—to measure and explore how our brains interact along these lines.

Involvement in Work Can Damage—or Build—Your Brain

For many working on detail-oriented challenges, such as with information technology, for example, working hours are, hopefully, neither too stressful nor particularly demanding of their decision-making skills. For the most part, they operate along the lines of what neuroscientists refer to as the "cognitive unconscious" or, in simpler terms, comfortable habit. Only when certain demands are made by unusual or unforeseen on-the-job circumstances are they challenged to bring their emotional awareness and interpersonal skills into play. But these circumstances and the responses to them determine whether or not they're acting with ConnectAbility.

Brain structure can be modified for better or worse. According to Emily Anthes, in an article published in *Scientific American Mind*, "Your behavior and environment can cause substantial rewiring of your brain or a reorganization of its functions." Ongoing stress at work, for example, can negatively affect the brain, particularly areas associated with emotions but even the thinking part as well. Even single events, according to one group of brain researchers reporting in the *Journal of Neuroscience*, if sufficiently intense, can alter the emotional part of the brain. Imagine what it might be like if, after 20 or so years of loyal devotion to your job, you're suddenly notified that your services are no longer needed. Armed security guards show up with grim faces and force you out of the building while your former associates gaze at you with unbelieving expressions on their faces. As you look back at your former "territory," your career flashes before your eyes. You might never be the same again and, according to the research, your brain might be altered forever.

On the other hand, positive experiences can alter our brains as well. Consider a great boss and wonderfully considerate and supportive associates. Our brains are actually able to change their physical wiring structure, according to research by Alvaro Pascual-Leone, neuroscientist at Harvard Medical School. It turns out, according to Sharon Begley, author of *Train Your Mind, Change Your Brain*, that "the adult brain retains impressive powers of 'neuroplasticity'—the ability to change its structure and function in response to experience." Daniel Siegel, author of *The Developing Mind*, has found that highly supportive relationships help build a better, healthier brain, both in terms of memory and more accurate intuition.

Make friends with your neighbors. Your brain can be altered by your work environment, for better or worse. For best effect, make sure you have good working relationships with your immediate associates.

PETs, CATs, and other "Power" Tools

We all know individuals who walk around as if they're looking for a fight. For whatever reason, they're always on edge, angry at the world and defending themselves against a threatening universe. Sure enough, there are many conflicts when individuals are ready to invite them into their lives. By the same token, we have also known their opposites—those who exude calmness and

Tips for Advancing Your ConnectAbility

- **If we can honor individual differences**, then it's likely the individuals will honor the overall welfare of the organization more conscientiously. There are two perspectives to getting things done through others—the hierarchy-based status approach and the more flexible chain of command in which sensitivity to individual differences is honored.
- **Using ConnectAbility to fine-tune our interactions with others**—listening, hearing, allowing ourselves to be authentic—can help build healthier brains, while feeling alienated and unappreciated over time can be harmful. According to scientific research, our brain structures continue to be affected—either positively or negatively—by our work environment.
- **Build dependably supportive relationships** with your associates at work. It's definitely worth your while.

seem to make others feel comfortable and safe. There is no conflict here, only solving problems in a caring, mindful manner. How can we account for such difference in personality?

The former is full of anger, ready to pounce on anyone who presents the slightest "offense." The latter appears to be happy with life, eager to assist others. While the first is likely to be in the habit of frowning, the second is usually seen smiling. In a global sense, the world is neutral, yet each of these two types arouses different reactions. Which would you choose?

If you would choose the second personality, then nurturing your authentic self and honoring what *is* rather than what *should be*—Awareness again—is the choice to make. Your real self is less ego-ridden (though not entirely ego-free), and consequently, you can more readily recognize what really is out there in the world, and others will be more in accord with your view. With less distortion by your needy and paranoid ego, you will see the world more clearly and others' worlds more objectively. As a result, you're more likely to feel in partnership with others rather than in competition against them, which means you're more disposed to helping them, not to mention allowing yourself to be supported. You can readily see how this would lead to more positive feelings about your work life in general.

Surprisingly, you feel a greater sense of self-esteem in part because you no longer doubt your own value in the face of other people. It's much easier to feel liked by others, even if nothing has changed in the outer world. But have patience. Others will be more drawn to you, especially as they get to spend time with you and your caring nature reveals itself. Whereas you may have felt lonely without the company of others before, now you'll enjoy being alone because you'll be more fulfilled by the time you do spend with others. The sense of loneliness will become foreign because the presence of friends will be more keenly felt, even in their absence. Put all this in the framework of business and you are now on your way to communicating more effectively with others, as well as becoming more productive in team efforts, more persuasive in sales or management, and a boost to company morale for those around you.

With the advent of medical technology, we can now begin to understand that emotions emanate from the brain as well as the heart. Words such as *PET* and *CAT* do not refer to the animal we stroke and love. They are acronyms for technical devices such as the positron emission tomography scanner and computerized axial tomography, alongside other medical tools such as fMRI (functional magnetic resonance imaging). Such tools, originally developed by pioneers Michael Phelps, Edward Hoffman, and Michael Ter-Pogossian back in 1973, allow us to understand how our brains interact at a social level, bringing about a greater comprehension of the interaction between the brains of people communicating with one another.

What is our business sense if not the consolidation of memory, habits both known and unknown, and the tendency to go one way or the other when it comes to making challenging business decisions? How can we find our business sense if not in the depths of our brain? Social science research has developed a new dependency on neuroscience, where PET scans and fMRIs reign supreme in discovering what makes us tick when it comes to our emotional and motivational selves.

The Balance of Brain Power

Neuroscience helps us understand how the overactive left frontal lobe (the thinking part of the brain) sometimes prevents the decision-making process—which involves the emotional parts of the brain—from being completed. Even Warren Buffett, whose Berkshire Hathaway investment entity turned a $1,000 investment into $27 billion during its lifetime, recognizes the need for more than intellectual analysis. "Investing is not a game where the guy with the 160 IQ beats the guy with a 130 IQ," he says in an interview published in *U.S. News & World Report*. "Once you have the ordinary intelligence, what you need is the temperament to control the urges that get other people into trouble in investing." This sounds very much like one of the components (Awareness of Context) of ConnectAbility.

Developments in scanning the brain gave birth to the neuroscience of ConnectAbility. We can now actually see pictures of how our brains operate and how they're affected by social interactions. The old school of psychology—in which the proponents of nature and nurture battle with one another—no longer stands. Genetics and experience blend to create the structural dynamics of our cerebral hemispheres. Now we can see much more precisely what happens in our brains as we conduct our lives at home, at school, and in business.

The Power of Authenticity

Our brain is a complex organ. The headline on how it works is that there is the old brain, evolved earlier, that deals primarily with emotions. The emerging news is the discovery of the importance of a small structure residing in both sides of the head—the amygdala—where we process new perceptions that might be threats, for example, all new people we meet, including new clients and customers. When the threat is great enough, we have "amygdala hijack," when the threatening information goes directly to the amygdalae, short-circuiting the thinking frontal cortex and resulting in "thoughtless" or irrational impulsive reaction.

We see this often in intense sports competition, in a very tightly fought game where tensions are running high. One athlete may earn a penalty for an overtly aggressive act in an intense moment, when the amygdala takes over and aggression is expressed. There is no thinking at that moment because the frontal cortex is left out of the loop. The athlete is likely to say, when confronted by a reporter after the game, "I was beside myself with anger." Teammates might say, "That's just not like him. He's just not that mean a person."

Think more broadly. Sometimes, following orders according to "the letter of the law" rather than the spirit intended for the benefit of the larger group can be hurtful and unproductive. Let your ConnectAbility have a go at it and make the decision that works for everyone, so that success is the outcome for all involved.

The aggressor's amygdala took over for the "usual" personality and something occurred that doesn't mesh with the thinking person's self-concept. This is the essence of amygdala hijack—impulsive, thoughtless reaction from the "old," emotionally based brain.

The other part, the new brain, more recently evolved, is where thought, planning, and mental control reside. Here, in the prefrontal cerebral cortex, just behind the forehead, we employ the skills of effective communication whenever the power of persuasion is called for (as in management, sales, production).

The research on social intelligence tells us that the most effective persuasion is done with authenticity. But, by definition, it cannot be faked, so pretending won't work. As Goleman puts it in an article from *Psychotherapy Networker*, "While we can intentionally try to mimic someone in order to foster closeness, such attempts tend to come off as awkward. Synchrony works best when it is spontaneous, not constructed from ulterior motives such as ingratiation or any other conscious intention." Simply trying to *appear* authentic is like the silly book title *The Five Rigid Steps to Natural Spontaneity*. It's an oxymoron.

So here's the obvious secret this technology offers us: to *appear* authentic on the business front, you must *be* authentic. You might allow the new brain, your thinking frontal cortex, to imagine yourself in the situation you're presenting to your audience and really *experience*—deeply—what you're attempting to convey. Don't hesitate to immerse yourself in the passion of your innermost feelings—others will follow suit. The result will be more successful and productive relationships.

A Brief Anatomy of the Brain

As we go through this section, the most important thing to know about the human brain is the distinction between how it affects knowing and feeling. The front of the brain—more specifically, the prefrontal cortex, behind the forehead—is the area in which most logical thinking takes place. This is where conscious decision making occurs. Feelings, on the other hand, are much more complex as far as brain anatomy is concerned. Feelings are likely to be generated both in the center of the brain, known as the limbic system, and in its connections with certain smaller structures in other parts, such as the amygdala.

For those who prefer a three-dimensional picture of the brain, consider a fist inside a boxing glove. The wrist represents the cerebellum (responsible for basic functions such as heartbeat, breathing, walking), the palm and fingers the emotional limbic system, and the glove itself the sensing and thinking cerebral cortex. The frontal cortex makes up about a third of the entire cortex.

It is widely accepted now that the right side of our frontal cortex, though only part of our consciousness, is more geared to creativity, spatiality, music, and the like, while the left portion provides logical function. This is an over-simplification, but it gives us an idea as to how the two parts of the frontal cortex—left and right—can interact optimally to provide the correct balance of intuition and logic. ConnectAbility, as we will see, involves the best cooperation between these two parts of the frontal cortex as well as between the entire frontal cortex and the emotional limbic system.

When we make business decisions, the areas of our brains that control logic and emotion work in tandem to produce a Desired Outcome. However, if we decide to operate from emotion alone, we'll have problems with social appropriateness, and if we operate from logic without any consideration of emotion, we'll have rigidity. ConnectAbility is the capacity to communicate with others using the appropriate balance of logic and emotion in making business decisions.

The Power to Create a New Reality

Now here's the interesting part: since the thinking section of the brain can override the fear-mongering amygdala just by focusing clearly and intently on the desired experience of our communication, then, admits neuropsychiatrist Dr. Richard Restak in his book *The Naked Brain*, "thanks to the frontal lobes of our brain, we have the power to create for ourselves [think facing your greatest business challenges here] a new and more empowering reality." Now we can engage our colleagues and customers with the substance and spirit of the image that we conjure up, as the business professionals we are, to experience that highly prized sense of authenticity and connection in our message. What emerging neuroscience research reveals is that whatever the mind imagines becomes its own reality. To complete the circle of powerful persuasion, it's necessary to be in touch with our audience at the emotional level. Here's where the two components of ConnectAbility—the Awareness and Performance Factors—come together to allow for the most effective transactions.

One of the more useful findings of emerging neuroscience data is how strongly we affect one another in our usual, day-to-day interactions. In research on macaque monkeys by University of Parma neuroscientist Giacomo Rizzolatti, it was discovered that the mere act of observing a certain action in others triggered the same neurons in the observer that would be required to imitate this very action. The neurons in the frontal cortex linking observer to observed were called "mirror neurons" by Rizzolatti and his colleagues.

Even more interesting, according to an article in *Science*, is the research done on humans by Marco Iacobini of UCLA in which he was able to cleverly separate perceived motivations on the part of the actors. When the film showed a hand moving toward a teacup in the context of enjoying the drink, there was much more activity in the mirror neurons of the observers than when watching the hand moving toward the same teacup in the context of cleaning up. Apparently, the perceived context of particular motivation plays a larger role at an unconscious level. Interestingly, these mirror neurons are activated not only by seeing, but also, according to the researchers, by hearing the sounds of certain actions in particular contexts, such as ripping paper to get to food.

Now how does this apply to business? Consider the salesman taking pen into hand as he aims toward the dotted line and then passing the pen on to the undecided prospect. Consider the presenter (addressing a board of directors or giving a talk from the platform) nodding his or her head while making a salient point. According to Goleman, in the same article from *Psychotherapy Networker* referenced earlier, "Human mirror neurons are far more flexible and diverse than those in monkeys, reflecting our sophisticated social abilities. . . . The human brain harbors multiple mirror neuron systems, not just for mimicking actions but also for reading intentions, for extracting the social implications from what someone does, and for reading emotions."

What we're discovering about mirror neurons in humans is that our body language and facial signals can communicate our intentions. And those signals enable us to influence others in an effective manner, particularly if we're genuine in our intentions. ConnectAbility is enhanced by this awareness. Our authenticity makes our communication much more acceptable to others. Mirror neurons in humans pick up on such subtleties and nuances. So if we're honest and authentic in our intentions, then ConnectAbility is well served—and highly effective. Whether it's team building or better sales outcomes, mirror neurons play their part.

In the days of the ancient Greeks, the term *mimesis*, which reflects the modern terms *mimic* or *imitate*, had a lot in common with our understanding of mirror neurons. In Plato's time, according to author Caleb Crain, writing in *The New Yorker*, "the word *mimesis* referred to an actor's performance of his role, an audience's identification with a performance, a pupil's recitation of his lesson, and an apprentice's emulation of his master." He goes on to say that Plato himself was concerned that all these situations could involve a "kind of trance or emotional enthrallment that came over people in all these situations." Even Plato could foresee the power of mirror neurons before such an understanding was even possible.

It's important to be more aware of how mirror neurons work with our colleagues and customers. Others can detect our perspectives, whether we're sincere or merely manipulative. Either one will be recognized—first at the unconscious level; soon after, at the conscious level. So it becomes clear that there's no point in pretending to be sincere; it has to "come from the heart."

The work before us is to integrate what we do at work with our own personal values and to put others' needs and considerations before our own as much as possible. When we do so effectively, then there is the "trance or emotional enthrallment," of which Plato speaks, that results in more successful outcomes.

The Neuroscience of Effective Business Communication

Some authors writing today seem to be convinced that if we imitate others in some physical, behavioral way—walking like them, adopting their expressions, reflecting their postures—then our empathy suddenly becomes superb. Another approach that has been around for decades is neurolinguistic programming (NLP), in which we're told that successful communication involves getting into the rhythm—breathing, speech patterns, sitting posture—of those we're trying to persuade. Now we have the neuroscientific data to validate such experience. As researcher Marco Iacobini puts it in a *New York Times* article, "The way we understand the emotions of other people is by simulating in our brain the same activity we have when we experience those emotions." Or as primatologist Frans de Waal at Emory University says in his book *Our Inner Ape*, "Try to mimic it a bit, and you will feel internally what other people feel." Now we can understand more clearly what Dale Carnegie meant when he said that it's easier to act your way into a feeling than to feel your way into action.

So, to communicate most effectively with our colleagues and customers in the workplace, we can reflect their posture and expressions, deeply and authentically "walk in their moccasins" to synchronize our brain patterns with theirs, and then get the highly desired rapport we seek. More than that, the research reveals that our audience, if we do the reflecting well, will echo those emotions in their own minds.

Emerging data also reveal that these "mirror" neurons cause others to feel and act like us, though not visibly, if we do our part effectively. This is one of the emotional components of ConnectAbility—primal awareness, occurring unconsciously in microseconds in both directions. According to neuroscientists Renate Motschnig-Pitrik and Michael Lux in an article from the Summer 2009 issue of the *Journal of Humanistic Psychology*, "mirror neurons support us in perceiving and feeling the inner world of persons with whom we are in contact on a conscious as well as subconscious level, to some degree even without conscious effort to do so." That's where the connection between speaker and listener comes full circle. As we engage in reflective experience (using the "inner voice" of our thinking frontal cortex to help us), the listeners, whether they choose to or not, immediately echo the very emotions we portray. By refining our skills, we can become much better communicators, more persuasive in our influence on others, and we can discover much more meaning in our work because of the connections we now enjoy.

If this sounds like artificial manipulation, think again, because what is being explored here is authentic communication—with our emotions open and honest—not lies and deception. ConnectAbility involves perceiving microexpressions of the face, which are impossible to fake; only by immersing ourselves in the conveyed emotion, authentically and with any associated vulnerability, will this process work effectively. The power of effective communication comes when we step back from the ongoing rush of business interaction. Then we can take stock of our own emotional vantage point "in the moment" and decide in which direction to move for the future success of the team or organization.

The "Technology" of Understanding Another's Point of View

To make clear the importance of ConnectAbility and how it differs from its sister concepts, emotional and social intelligence, let's revisit the distinction. Emotional intelligence deals with four components: emotional self-awareness, self-control (of disturbing and distracting emotions), empathy, and management of interpersonal relations.

Social intelligence, with its focus on the research of neuroscience and human interaction, is primarily focused on social awareness through listening and empathy, as well as success in social relationships, including influencing others through appropriate self-presentation. Social intelligence has proven a human characteristic that is distinct from general intelligence, though there is certainly a degree of overlap between the two.

ConnectAbility applies all the structure and research of its sister concepts and takes that into the world of business interaction. Its focus is clearly on the dynamics that involve business interaction—understanding both colleagues and customers (the Awareness Factor) and, second, making the best business presentation possible to the target group (the Performance Factor).

Reading others well, including their emotional disposition, is the skill of putting ourselves into someone else's shoes—whether that be customer or colleague—while listening attentively. This business-oriented form of empathy (listening skills) is the delicate yet powerful option of allowing mental images and/or emotional sensations of shared experiences to emerge within. It involves:

- Listening to another's story
- A basic understanding of emotions—hurt, sorrow, anger, and so forth
- Allowing this inner feeling to grow without judgment
- Framing this feeling within the context of the particular business situation at hand
- Responding with a question, to make sure what we've heard the other person sharing is on target in terms of emotional accuracy

But reading others successfully also involves accessing our own emotions to accurately capture someone else's emotion. According to Dr. Tobin Hart, from his article "The Refinement of Empathy" appearing in the *Journal of Humanistic Psychology*, this occurs by comparing what your colleagues or customers are telling you with your own experience, to arrive at a similar emotional experience.

The Right Balance for the Best Business

Emotions come from the limbic system, roughly at the center of the brain, but the conscious *awareness* of any emotions involves the "thinking" frontal cortex. So we can't be aware of any emotion unless the limbic system and frontal cortex are working in conjunction with one another. We feel emotional awareness (Awareness Factor), one of the two key components of ConnectAbility, usually without much control over it, but we can't communicate such awareness (Performance Factor) without first engaging our frontal cortex to find the right words. In general, we have some degree of control over our emotions, but we can choose to have greater control over how we express them in a business setting, if we so desire. The other component of ConnectAbility is the management of our communication of feelings and emotions (communication skills) for the best outcome of our business.

Too much emotion and we're likely to be ostracized or, at best, a poor performer at work. Too little emotion (or ignoring emotion entirely) and we're likely to be seen by our colleagues and customers as rigid and inflexible, unable to make good decisions involving people. Those in sales or management can well appreciate the need to have the right balance of intellect and emotion. We can't very well control our emotions too closely, but we can definitely control how we express them.

Ultimately, it's the sensitive interplay of the awareness of our ongoing interactions—at any particular moment (Awareness of Influence), along with the social awareness of the right way to handle those emotions (Awareness of Others), given the business context we find ourselves in (Awareness of Context)—that creates the power of ConnectAbility. For example, successful sales involve a sensitive awareness of the customers' needs in the various stages of selling a product or idea, from opening to closing. Therefore, selling with ConnectAbility involves:

- Listening before speaking (Awareness of Others)
- Letting the customers lay the groundwork to clarify their needs so we understand them deeply (Awareness of Context), and only then,

- Demonstrating a genuine understanding of their needs (listening skills), and
- Presenting a warmly persuasive attitude and doing what's necessary to satisfy the customer (presentation skills)

The Anatomy of a Winning Business Mind

The anatomy of memory is complex, but not too difficult to remember. Most researchers divide memory into two categories: **explicit** memory—consisting of the known details of your life—and **implicit** memory—involving, for example, physical movements such as skill in writing on the keyboard. Yet there are two types of explicit memory: **autobiographical** memory—recording the experiences themselves (what we commonly refer to as memory)—and **semantic** memory—learned patterns of behavior that come with experience.

So what does this mean for us business folk? For one thing, it reveals to us the beginnings of the complexity of a good business mind. Why do some individuals succeed so brilliantly and make a lot of money while others struggle through long hours and dedicate themselves, yet remain mired in menial jobs? For example, how do we understand that CEOs of large corporations demand and receive millions of dollars for putting in roughly the same week's worth of time that the rest of us do for mere thousands? This new perspective of memory begins to shed light on this long-standing issue.

How CEOs Earn Their Salaries

The leaders whom we both admire and envy, in most cases, possess an elegant combination of drive, confidence, intellect, and memory, highlighted most often with at least a dash of good luck. All of these factors play their part, but our focus on memory is new. Autobiographical memory we understand quite clearly; it's semantic memory that fascinates. Making the right decisions for a multimillion-dollar corporation requires a memory for complex financial and business patterns that have a place in the experience of the decision maker. So what works is the right combination of all the factors mentioned above with a superior semantic memory based on having faced challenges similar to the ones that might be forthcoming.

In other words, those successful individuals with high-paying salaries and added perks deserve them because they're among the very few who have had the opportunity to be exposed to challenging business decisions similar to the ones they will face, and have the semantic memory to generalize from their experience. Drawing on their experience, such leaders of industry can focus clearly on the relevant aspects of ongoing challenges without being overly distracted by the individual details. When they do their job effectively, they can separate the wheat from the chaff more efficiently than their support staff. If they fail, then the boards they report to will make their own decisions, hopefully based on a collective semantic memory.

In addition to a superior semantic memory relevant to the decisions at hand, a CEO with ConnectAbility also has the challenge of communicating such decisions not only to the board but also to staff members, shareholders at public meetings, and the media when public statements are called for. When Robert Nardelli left Home Depot in early 2007, it became clear that his success at improving the company's bottom line was not enough to overcome his challenge to communicate effectively. Where persons in lesser positions can get by with average communication skills, the CEOs of well-known companies cannot afford such mediocrity—they must be superior. Rather than one brain communicating with another, the highly visible CEO must keep in mind how one brain can communicate with thousands. The brain with superior semantic memory must also have the skill of communicating with a multitude of other discerning brains. There is little room for error.

The Ultimate Game

The neuroscience of ConnectAbility also tells us quite a bit about how we persuade others and negotiate with one another in financial transactions. At the

Tips for Advancing Your ConnectAbility

- **Learn the "secret" to increasing sales.** It's the scientific approach of going step-by-step from listening (Awareness Factor) to fulfilling a need (Performance Factor) in a highly systematic fashion.
- **Increase the success factor in your career arc.** Roughly speaking, there are two aspects of memory: (a) facts and figures and (b) patterns of behavior based on experience. The more familiar you are with patterns of behavior in terms of business experience, the more likely you'll be successful (and rewarded) with increased responsibility.
- **Understand how your brain handles complex undertakings.** With proper understanding you'll become more successful as you allow the brain to do its job. Our brains respond in a very complex yet intelligent manner to difficult challenges, all on a subconscious level.

Center for the Study of the Brain, Mind, and Behavior at Princeton University, Dr. Jonathan Cohen and his colleagues study game theory—more specifically, ultimate games.[2] In one research paradigm, two players are involved, one giving the other an ultimatum.

For example, you and Frank are given $100 on the following condition: Frank decides how the money will be divided between you and him and proposes that plan to you. If you agree, then Frank gets the money and it is divided accordingly. If you reject the plan, neither of you gets the money. So Frank has to try to come up with a sharing plan that gives him the most money yet enough to satisfy you so that you won't reject his proposal.

You should be happy with any amount, since even $1 is better than nothing. But human nature is such that most people in your position refuse to accept the ultimatum if it's "insultingly" low. For example, if Frank decided to share only $30 out of $100, most people would reject such a proposal. They'd rather get nothing than feel they're being treated so unfairly. Then both lose out. That makes more subjective sense than logical sense—and that's human nature.

But put in terms of social evolution, if you were joining a new group, your status would depend, to a large extent, on your ability to display power over others, which is largely manifested in terms of gratification of needs. If you settle for a smaller proportion in an ultimate game, you're not as likely to garner respect. However, as time and the game go on, early refusals of smaller shares—resulting in no "income"—give way to the proposer offering you larger shares in order to make the game work—to keep you as a working member in the group.

In other words, if you refuse smaller portions, at first you get nothing, but neither does Frank, since both players have to agree for the proposition to work. Over time, Frank learns to respect your demands for a higher share and eventually an equilibrium arises in which you get more than originally offered, Frank learns that doing so is the only way to go, and a healthy relationship is formed. This will work out satisfactorily only if you are willing to refuse a small offer initially, even if you make nothing on that initial offer. Awareness of Context trumps commonsense, linear logic. This helps explain why the human brain tends to refuse the small offer even though it doesn't make economic sense for that transaction alone.

The underlying importance of the research described in this section is the radical notion that we affect one another in ways never before understood. If you and I have any business or working relationship at all, then what each of us does affects the other much more directly than we ever realized. Imagine what that means to individuals working together on a daily basis. Imagine what that means to a boss trying to influence the workforce he or she manages. Imagine what that means to the leaders of industry as they influence and persuade those in their organizations to follow visions of financial success. Finally, imagine what that means in terms of the neuroscience of negotiations and marketing. There's no turning back from this new power of ConnectAbility.

The Benefits of Awareness

Greater emotional awareness of our own feelings and of those around us can preempt the terrible consequences of "unheard" emotional pain, sometimes even more effectively than medications. As emotional awareness becomes a greater part of our culture, there is a much better chance of mollifying the deep pain of extreme jealousy or grief before it leads to such drastic reactions as homicide or suicide.

The ramifications for the workplace are enormous. We either make use of this emerging knowledge or ignore it at our own peril. As competitive as the workplace has become, the companies that choose to ignore such knowledge and cocoon themselves in a system of closed hierarchical thinking operate according to what we refer to as the hierarchy-based Status Factor. On the other hand, those who operate with openness to their environment—and the humans within it—operate according to the hierarchy-independent Awareness Factor.

In a fascinating area of genetic research, scientists have begun to uncover the possibility that we're genetically disposed to be aligned to either the Status or Awareness Factor. "These views are deep-seated and built into our brains," according to Rice University political scientist John Alford in an issue of *NewScientist*. Different patterns of brain activity for the two types are being explored by neuroscientists. After two decades of work on behavioral genetics, including a huge database of the political opinions of 30,000 twins from Virginia, Alford also found that "identical twins were more likely than non-identical twins to give the same answers to political questions."

Are there genes that determine whether we're more aligned with the Awareness as opposed to the Status Factor? This might be possible, according to the research of University of California political scientist James Fowler published in the same issue of the *NewScientist*. Fowler discusses two well-studied genes "which both help control the levels of serotonin, a neurotransmitter that also influences brain areas linked with trust and social interaction. People with versions of the genes that are better at regulating serotonin tend to be more sociable." Trust and disposition to social interaction sound more like Awareness Factor than Status Factor. Does that mean that these genes characterize awareness?

What about a Status Factor gene? At the April 2007 annual conference of the Midwest Political Science Association held in Chicago, University of Illinois professor Ira Carmen revealed his studies of the D_4DR gene, which involves regulation of the neurotransmitter dopamine. Professor Carmen put forth the possibility that "dopamine might therefore be linked to the need to impose order on the world."

In a study of 65 individuals at Northwestern University published in a March 2009 issue of *Parade* magazine, men and women were given money to invest, choosing between risky and more cautious options. Those with the high-dopamine genes put their money in high-risk investments 25 percent more often while those with high-serotonin genes invested 28 percent less money in risky investments. Altogether, said one of the researchers, genes probably account for "less than 30 percent of the variation in risk-taking

Tips for Advancing Your ConnectAbility

- **Pay attention to your relationships at work.** Research on the human mind reveals that we're much more influenced by one another than we ever imagined.
- **Have someone listen to your concerns before they become too heavy to handle.** An awareness of emotional states helps to prevent the extremes of anxiety, depression, or other discomforts that might interfere with work.
- **ConnectAbility offers flexibility for respecting individual differences at the expense of rigid rule obeisance.** Ultimately, a rough division of values in the workplace breaks down to hierarchy-based status values versus a somewhat less rigid, cooperative structure, allowing for greater flexibility in the interpretation of rules.

behavior." So that leaves plenty of influence due to cultural factors, emerging news on the investments, and individual experience.

In the remaining chapters, we'll explore ConnectAbility even further. We'll look at the venture of applying scientific discoveries from the framework of multiple intelligences to the world of business, and how the emerging values and proven benefits of the Awareness and Performance Factors can enhance our organizations.

CHAPTER 3

Flowing and Connecting

KEY 3: MATCH SKILLS WITH POTENTIAL

In developing strong partnerships with your colleagues and customers, do whatever you can to ensure your skills (or those of individuals under your management) are matched with tasks or responsibilities that tap your (or their) potential. When a challenge just barely exceeds the skill level of an individual, you get "flow"—the highest level of productivity. Just make sure to close the loop of ConnectAbility by communicating your appreciation in a way that makes the most sense to your colleague.

MIHALY CSIKSZENTMIHALYI, AUTHOR of the books *Flow* and *Good Business*, describes "flow" (a term he coined) as being so challenged by a project and successful in meeting the challenge that time flows by unnoticed. It's what we feel as we complete a job that challenges the very talents we're most confident of, like an artist painting a bucolic scene on a warm afternoon in the country or a musician attacking a piano piece that she mastered to perfection. There is almost an absence of time in that the individual gets so carried away by his or her involvement that nothing else matters. There is a joyful sense of being part of the process of whatever is being accomplished or created—time literally flows, as everything else disappears, except for a focus on the ongoing activity. This same concept can be applied to your job as well. "Anything can be enjoyable if the elements of flow are present," writes Csikszentmihalyi in *Flow*. "Within that framework, doing a seemingly boring job can be a source of greater fulfillment than one ever thought possible."

No matter how intricate or simple your job is, if the components are right then flow can exist. What's crucial is that the challenge *just* meet the skill involved—only then can a magical connection between the external world and our inner consciousness occur. It's as if all previous experience led up to these special moments, when task and human response become intertwined in a seamless circuit.

Choosing Your Joy

If you have any choice in the matter of how you spend your working time, then your best bet, in terms of enjoying your work, is to do what you enjoy so much that you'd do it even if you never got paid. Your first thought might be something that you know does not pay enough to live on, but that doesn't mean you can't find a well-paying job that still fills your needs.

For those of us who are in more conventional work settings (as opposed to creative professions, such as artists, actors, musicians, professional athletes, and so forth) there are still choices. As time goes by, we can get a sense of which aspects of our jobs are most enjoyable. We can lean in those directions over time in terms of learning more about them, volunteering for projects that attract us, and not getting sidetracked by monetary temptations.

Go with the flow. Explore what aspect of your work "flows" into meaning and joy. Focus on it.

In a Gallup poll of 5.4 million employees at 474 organizations, American workers were asked how happy they were at work. The results revealed that only 29 percent felt engaged in their work. More than half reported not being engaged, and 16 percent felt actively disengaged. In Germany, only half as many felt engaged; in Singapore, only one-third. These statistics were not substantially affected by either the dot-com boom or its devastating subsequent bust. Apparently, feeling engaged or disengaged in work is a deeper phenomenon that is not easily moved by swings in the economy.

Interestingly, one of the most critical questions in the Gallup poll was "Do you have a best friend at work?" Another was "Does your supervisor or someone else at work care about you as a person?" There are basic human needs to be met at work as much as at home. The first of the two questions turned out to be highly correlated with profitability and involvement with customers. The second question would seem to correlate with job satisfaction naturally, since there's a great need to feel cared about as a person regardless of the context of the situation. According to psychologist Abraham Maslow, known for his Hierarchy of Needs, feeling appreciated as a person is a primal need. So being cared about as a person at work, whether by a supervisor or someone else, would result in greater involvement. It appears that connecting with others at work is a significant need. ConnectAbility helps fill that need.

Over the years, it's become much clearer that money is not a top motivator—it's just the easiest to count. We're learning, over time, that the meaningful aspects of work have much more to do with feeling appreciated for our efforts than how much we bring home in our pockets. Meaning also comes from the challenge of dealing with new situations. It's the newness or variety in work that makes it meaningful and pleasurable. According to Dr. Gregory Berns, in an interview quoted in *The Sunday Paper*, "Understanding that the pleasure money confers is significantly increased by the work done to earn it turns upside down a basic tenet of economics—that work is a negative and money is a positive. I think it is the other way around." But it's much easier to talk about money than it is about wanting to feel appreciated. So money remains the superficial currency of human value in the marketplace.

If that's the case, then what's so special about the privilege of staying at home and telecommuting? Truth is there may be a problem there. There is a deep, pervasive need to connect with others on a daily basis. Working at home may be convenient in terms of comfort and flexibility, but it doesn't do much for feeling connected with others in the flesh. There's something about the structure of traveling to a place where there are others to share a workspace, and interact on a social basis, that is highly meaningful. That awareness in itself gives you a leg up on making your work more meaningful and enjoyable.

Another factor in happiness at work has to do with the battle against routine. The old Hawthorne studies done at the Western Electric Company in Cicero, Illinois, in the 1920s gave birth to what's become known as the Hawthorne effect: it's not the types of changes in the work environment that bring about increases in productivity but rather the actual process of change itself. For example, if you increase lighting or decrease lighting, productivity will increase, at least for a while. It's not the degree of lighting that makes the difference. What really brings about the rise in productivity is the attention that comes with change—any change. The social factor of getting more attention far outweighs any physical factors.

The most outstanding factor is that of a sense of belonging. Meaning comes from the feeling that we play an important role in the mission of the organization. That meaning comes from around us—our bosses and co-workers. If we feel they value our contribution, then the meaning is assured. How does the boss communicate that? Conventionally, in the form of accurate and supportive reviews, occasional notes of appreciation for jobs well done, public comments in appreciation of our efforts. At a more subtle level, there are private comments or mention in a memo going off to a third party.

Feedback from co-workers is much more complex. Issues of competition, jealousy, the sociology of small group spinoffs, and so forth, are always in the air. What filters through all this grapevine of feedback ends up feeling either positive or negative; there's little middle ground. For the most part, we can expect a positive feeling if we're doing our job and not hurting anyone in the process. Personality differences being what they are, it's not unusual for an individual or group to begin to form an opinion about someone in particular who may call attention to him- or herself, sometimes for no bad reason, for example, by being particularly good-looking or harder working than most.

That's where the "best friend" dynamic plays a significant role. A good friend will keep you informed of any incipient rumors that may harm you, keep you abreast of the latest political changes that might affect you, and listen to your version of inadvertent conflicts in which you may be part. That best friend is like an insurance policy against being socially ostracized. It's a protective bumper in your career arc as you come up against unexpected challenges.

Creating Fulfillment at Work

A highly energetic president at a telecommunications company—let's call him Jack—works hard with problems on a daily basis. The work becomes overwhelming as the weeks and months go by with no one to lean on, especially with the more challenging breakdowns in morale as a difficult economy forces increased layoffs. He feels overburdened and completely unappreciated. His board chair invites him to lunch and informs him how much he is appreciated by the rest of the board. Jack is encouraged, but he needs more. What else can he do to use his ConnectAbility to create a more meaningful and productive work environment? Here are some ideas:

- Become a more active resource for the VPs under him. There's something about being of service to others—colleagues, not customers, in this case—that makes a job much more meaningful. There's nothing like becoming a resource to others to do away with the sense of isolation that can come from working alone.
- Finding a mentor can add loads of meaning to any job. A trusted mentor has likely been there before, wherever "there" is. Jack can be on the look-

Lead with concern. If you're in a position of leading others, encourage them with courteous and authentic interest so they feel appreciated.

out for a more experienced, senior executive while attending conferences or other business meetings.

■ If a mentor is hard to find, find a small group of peers to create a private support group. Meeting monthly or weekly with this master group allows Jack to air out what seem like irrational grievances, in other words, to vent. There's nothing like letting the air out of your accumulated frustrations to feel refreshed and more prepared to take on the next day's trials.

■ Hire a coach. Finding a formal coach in whom Jack can put his trust and with whom he could share his self-doubts can be daunting, given the fish-bowl nature of high-level executives. More informal coaching can be had by trading off with another peer. The essence of coaching is the process of accountability. Using his friendly charm, Jack scouts out a leader from another organization who thinks like him and would also benefit from this best-friend working relationship—another win-win resolution. He and a partner can commit to overcoming a particular challenge and hold one another accountable. The sense of professional growth at his own initiative can add substantial meaning to his job as well as to his "accounting" partner.

All these choices give Jack a greater sense of control over his career, and a sense of control is what adds meaning to his work. Over the years, psychologists have found that optimists have a greater sense of control over their lives than pessimists. Since the sense of control may be exaggerated, it's sometimes referred to as the "illusion of control." But illusion or not, it's what makes us feel better and our jobs more meaningful; whether we actually have all the control we feel is a moot point. In actuality, the more control we feel,

Get feedback. If you're in a place of wanting more accurate feedback about yourself, make a connection with a peer who thinks like you and in whom you can confide, that is, practice being your authentic self.

the more control we exercise, even though there may be a factor of "luck" involved as well.

Since friendship and social support are so important to meaning at the job, it should not be surprising that emotional intelligence with its emphasis on interpersonal openness has become so popular in many circles. Above all, emotional intelligence competencies have to do with emotional authenticity and empathy. This offers a broad brush to paint all relationships with a friendly coat. Authenticity in leadership has become in vogue because of this as well, since the leader of any organization sets the tone.

Authentic Leadership

Why would top leaders want to be authentic with the risk of yielding some of their authoritarian power? Because happiness pays! Up to 25 percent of excellence in job performance depends on employee happiness. That's a lot of productivity, not to be sneezed at when figuring the bottom line. In one study at St. Lucie Medical Center in South Florida, when nursing teams were adjusted according to the personality strengths of the individuals, turnover was reduced by 65 percent, and patient satisfaction increased measurably.

Authentic styles of leadership encourage self-awareness and sensitivity as to how management is perceived. Any boss who knows how he or she comes across is more apt to make decisions that are more acceptable to the staff members and therefore increase employee satisfaction. That sets a tone for

Find a partner. If you're involved in a challenging project and falling behind, find an associate who will hold you accountable in a friendly way and return the favor. That's finding a coach for free—another win-win situation.

staff members to be open as well, and conflict and resistance give way to more effective team effort and better overall results.

Increasing Your Team's Sense of Fulfillment at Work

So what are some specific steps to accomplish this sense of fulfillment or satisfaction that will lead to improved bottom-line results? And, more to the point, how does a boss encourage his or her team to overcome what initially seems like a paradox—assuring good output while at the same time maintaining personal meaning and satisfaction on everyone's part? If you're responsible for a team and you want to accomplish this, here are some recommendations:

- Make sure all team members under you get the sense of how much you appreciate their work. One way is by communicating a sense of the big picture. Let's say, for example, that a team member, let's call her Carrie, is doing lab research on cancer prevention. Though her work is highly meaningful by anybody's standards—mixing, measuring, and analyzing solutions all day, working with lab mice and tissue samples—it can easily become routine and dull. Without regular feedback as to its place in the larger scheme, such work could begin to take on a sense of drudgery. If you can make sure Carrie sees the big picture of so many lives being saved and the many families that would avoid the misery of cancer in a family member, Carrie would find the meaning that might otherwise evade her.
- Remember to treat each of your team members with the courtesy of asking about his or her family. Nothing else with so little effort will go as far to make employees feel part of the organization. They'll go from feeling like numbers to feeling recognized as the human beings they are. At the same time, keep your antennae up for the possibility that some people like to keep their business and personal lives separate. Don't paint all individuals with the same broad strokes.
- Try to find positive incidents to compliment your staff members rather than limiting your feedback to correcting mistakes. More than anything else, research in psychology has taught us that rewarding good behavior is much more effective than punishing mistakes.

■ Even during tough times, when budgets are lean and job security is at low ebb, treat your staff members with care and their loyalty will be assured when the economic roller coaster starts climbing back up. Turnover is becoming an increasing challenge for management. Loyalty is in scarce supply, but those whom you treat with dignity in hard times are much more likely to remain loyal during better times.

■ Stay in touch with your key team members in terms of how they feel on a regular basis. We all have our ups and downs. Be "in the moment" with them—if you notice a dramatic shift in their mood or behavior, get involved. Find out what's happening now, not next week when you might have more time or at the upcoming review just a few weeks away. Again, if you feel they prefer their privacy, honor that as well. You may have to use more sensitive means to help them, such as inviting them to come into your office when they feel the need rather than inviting them at your convenience.

■ See each team member as a unique resource with special abilities. No one has all the characteristics necessary for excellence in all corners. Each person has his or her strengths and weaknesses. Become more sensitive to using the positive resources that do exist; group individuals with complementary strengths for the most productive teams.

■ Let your deeper self shine through to your staff members. If you happen to be more introverted than you like, no problem—just have quiet chats in private, and let the other person guide the conversation. Whatever your personality, don't hide behind your desk, metaphorically speaking. Charisma is, in part, letting others know what you really stand for and making the commitment to lead others with that banner waving freely in the wind.

Stay aware of what's under the surface. Stay aware of others' feelings. Just as a ship's use of radar avoids low-lying icebergs, your awareness can be used to pick out and avoid emotional turmoil and even potential tragedy before they become sad reality.

It Ain't the Money

When it comes to using ConnectAbility to add meaning and fulfillment to our lives, there is another source that may be surprising to some—religion and spirituality. Thousands of articles have been published over the years that come to this same conclusion. What is interesting here is that those in organized religion as well as free-spirited agnostics can benefit from these findings. It is not only those who attend church or temple who benefit; it's also those who have a strong sense of spirituality. The bottom line is that, by identifying with a larger entity than oneself, one's life becomes enlarged. That larger entity could even be a humanitarian cause such as cancer prevention or a commitment to ecological welfare. Either way, one's personal problems are diminished when one feels part of something larger.

Identifying with a group, whether it be a house of worship or others with commitment to a common cause, automatically brings friendship and support and certainly a sense of community, so helpful in adding meaning to one's life.

If you are proud of your employer and feel that the organization is doing something meaningful—helping associates as in Jack's case, doing research to prevent disease in Carrie's case—then that commitment to help others can serve as the larger cause, adding meaning and joy to work. If a sense of compassion can be added to the process, then there is additional meaning to the whole work effort. The same can be said for how a sense of commitment to colleagues and customers can be equally rewarding.

Awareness-Based Medical Practice

ConnectAbility is just as important in professional private practice as it is in corporate environments. Those medical doctors with ConnectAbility, for example, have much better relationships with their patients. According to a study reported in a 2008 issue of *Medical Education*, nurse-rated measures of awareness skills of the doctors for whom they worked were positively associated with their patients' trust of them. In other words, the higher the doctors' awareness skills, the better the doctor-patient relationships.

Among medical specialists in the United States, the Awareness Factor benefits not only patients but doctors as well. According to one study, medical doctors who lack the Awareness Factor are much more likely to get sued for malpractice. "What comes up again and again in malpractice suits," writes Malcolm Gladwell in his bestselling book *Blink*, "is that patients say they were rushed or ignored or treated poorly."

To determine what the difference was between surgeons who were sued for malpractice at least twice and those who hadn't been sued at all, Wendy Levinson and her colleagues recorded hundreds of conversations between surgeons and their patients. What they found was a small but remarkable difference. Those who weren't sued, it turned out, spent somewhat more time with their patients and, even more important, were much more likely to be experienced as empathetic and understanding. They engaged in active listening and were more likely to share something humorous.

Both groups gave equal amounts of medical information, so the difference was the Awareness Factor in their communication—listening in the moment to really hear the experience of each patient. Surely, the other surgeons were professional and gave good treatment. Hopefully, they liked their patients and cared about them as well. But the doctors with ConnectAbility cared more—enough to spend a bit of extra time and to come across as more concerned. There was no indication of any difference between the two groups in terms of experience or skill in surgical practice, merely the difference in the skills of awareness-based listening.[1]

Return on Investment—"Mind-Boggling"

To explore even further the details of this research, Nalini Ambady and her colleagues selected two 10-second clips from each surgeon for analysis. She "content-filtered" the slices to remove the high-frequency sounds, ensuring that the surgeons' voices were unintelligible. The resulting garble was analyzed for such characteristics as dominance, hostility, and warmth.

Using a blind procedure, the sued surgeons could be differentiated from their unsued colleagues just by the degree to which they sounded dominant, a quality associated with the hierarchy-dependent Status Factor. According to

Malcolm Gladwell, who interviewed Ms. Ambady for his book *Blink*, "Malpractice sounds like one of those infinitely complicated and multidimensional problems. But in the end it comes down to a matter of respect . . . through tone of voice." Had these "dominant" doctors invested some of their time in learning awareness listening skills, their return on investment would have been mind-boggling.

Medical schools are beginning to come to grips with the Awareness Factor. In the past few years, more and more schools have begun to offer courses on this subject, including components such as empathy and compassionate care. "We have to prepare the next generation of doctors differently—they can't be just walking textbooks," said David Leach, executive director of the Accreditation Council for Graduate Medical Education, in an article in the *Wall Street Journal*. At Southern Illinois University Medical School, for instance, medical students are offered a course called Empathy 101.

Taking Charge

But empathy is only part of the process. Another major aspect has to do with self-expression.

Mike had been downright depressed about his job: he'd been overlooked for a well-deserved promotion and just wasn't feeling appreciated. It left him down and dismal. Then we began to talk and, using the principles of the Awareness Factor, brought to light the true qualities he had to offer that he hadn't been aware of.

At times, there was personal challenge. He was beginning to feel more accountable to himself about how he was moving ahead. He began to look at himself more realistically and, over time, it felt better to know how he came across to others more completely, more honestly. He had to admit some negative things about himself, about not being open to negative feedback in the past. He sometimes felt a tension between the more comfortable, older, head-in-the-sand approach and his emerging real self, more open to who he was, more open to others' assessments of him, more open to the challenges that lay before him. Was he ready to take them on? At the end of the day, he felt a deep satisfaction at taking charge of his life and moving forward in a more confident manner.

Mike was eyeing what he could only describe as an "alternate universe," from which he was able to convert self-defeating energy to more constructive self-empowerment. As he became more open to feedback and to gaining control over his destiny, he saw himself as more competitive, assertive, as compared with his "old" self. He became adept at serving his own needs toward job satisfaction, to advance himself with the help of others. He was able to blend his chosen area of expertise with the needs of the organization. He became more responsive to those needs as well as to his own.

Our discussions uncovered the confidence that had been buried and necessary to have an open-hearted talk with his boss. That talk turned his career around. Not only did he get a promotion but it was a "double" promotion, getting him a position a level higher than he expected. Now his career truly has an arc that bears watching. Mike is a happy man who finds much more meaning in his work, and he's earning much more as well. Making your job more enjoyable is certainly an attractive feature for most—if not all—people who work for a living.

"Noble Heart" Over Driving Ego

What makes work enjoyable is the same across all work settings. It has to do with finding your work meaningful and challenging. Finding it meaningful has to do with feeling a degree of control over it—and being appreciated for your efforts. It has to do with feeling you're in the right place for what you have to offer. And that doesn't come easily. Sometimes, as in Mike's case, it takes half a career to find all these factors coming together. Some fortunate individuals find it fairly early in their careers; others may be so unfortunate as to never discover it in their working life.

The application of ConnectAbility is not always easily described. It has, in part, to do with authenticity in the moment, the awareness of making responsible choices from existing options, looking at what is now possible within a context of limitations, and searching for win-win outcomes. It has to do with taking the ego out of the driver's seat and replacing it with what the Tibetans call "noble heart."

Let's take a closer look at that term. Among other things, nobility has to do with high character, generosity, and exceptional qualities, with grand appearance and lofty ideals. More than mere empathy, noble heart involves taking the long view for others as well as yourself. It means revealing your intentions so as to pave the way for others to decide whether or not they're ready to follow. It means being ready to reveal your character so that others may choose what you mean to them. All this gives shape to the essence of ConnectAbility

The end effect of this concept is that you begin to feel more fulfillment at work because you've chosen to involve deeper aspects of yourself. Whatever your job, whatever the level of responsibility, whatever the nature of your work setting, you and you alone can choose how much candor, integrity, and awareness there will be in your day-to-day job. This is not a simple process, not a magic bullet for happiness at work, not without much effort to dislodge your stubborn ego. And the job of getting there is never completed—because your ego is still necessary, even when it's invited to take a backseat. That ego will make itself known, time and again, and well it should—none of us can survive without it. But now it's in a servant rather than master role—most of the time, if you can manage it.

To the extent you can enter the process of facing your real self with the Awareness Factor, your work will become not only more meaningful, satisfying, and enjoyable, but also *easier*. This aspect has to do with such total involvement in doing your work that you occasionally enter what athletes refer to as "the zone." You become so enjoyably engrossed in your work that time just *is*—it simply flies by.

Risk Doesn't Sell, and Fear Doesn't Lead

One of the best exercises conducted over the years involving emotional intelligence consists of asking participants to differentiate between good and bad bosses. No matter where this question is asked, the answers are very similar. Bad bosses are described as being self-centered and arrogant and acting like bullies. Good bosses are invariably described as being good listeners and sensitive to others' feelings and demonstrating democratic values. According to Tom Rath, author of *Vital Friends*, in an article from *Performance*, "These great managers care about each of their employees as a real human being, not just as a means to an end."

A good coach, in our experience, raises the morale of the team by showing confidence in team spirit, specifically by sticking to his or her lineup even when there may be occasional losses. A poor coach, on the other hand, punishes players by benching them when they perform poorly. Such players always have failure on their minds because they know they'll be singled out as soon as they make a mistake. They may perform well for a while, but when the pressure builds they tend to fold.

Similarly, in the workplace, a good boss focuses on the positive, giving his or her subordinates the benefit of the doubt, offering support, even when mistakes are made, as long as they're a basis for learning. A bad boss tends to punish any mistake, believing that learning takes place by focusing on errors. Even though professional athletes make money even if they occasionally mess up, what's important to them is their self-esteem and the esteem of their teammates. Similarly in the workplace, such concern about esteem, or loss of it, can make an associate choke under pressure, causing a loss of confidence. The Awareness Factor boss encourages his or her subordinates, building their confidence and group loyalty. The boss lacking awareness takes subordinates to task for any apparent error, creating a sense of anxiety and fear throughout the organization resulting in higher turnover, decreased zeal, and lower productivity.

I Relate, Therefore I Win

Since business is made up of transactions between and among people, the most significant aspect has to do with facing what is really going on within yourself and others.

The authoritarian point of view is driven by a dispassionate execution of the "business as usual" rules dictated with formal rigidity. This hierarchy-based model contrasts sharply with ConnectAbility, which takes a collabora-

Tips for Advancing Your ConnectAbility

- **Bring a sense of commitment to the job**—whether in some form of spiritual connection or in seeing the bigger picture of the contribution resulting from your work.
- **Invest the time and energy to nurture at least one or two close friendships.** Otherwise, the sense of isolation is damaging both to the individual as well as to job performance.
- **It's all about the people**, more specifically, appreciation of people and their unique contributions.

tive approach, stemming from a supportive, nurturing perspective focused on service, cultural excellence, and leading with caring and trust. Taking the AK rifle from the monastery, as discussed in Chapter 2, was done on principle, acquiescing to military authority, even though facing the reality of the situation made it clear that this group of Christians would be completely at the mercy of the hoodlums surrounding them, at least some of whom might be fanatics or terrorists.

ConnectAbility is based on relationship, what is fair to both sides, whereas the authoritarian approach ignores anything other than selfish point of view. Awareness builds rapport and trust, ultimately alliance. The French philosopher Rene Descartes illustrated the division between mind and body by declaring in his *Discours de la Methode*, "I think, therefore I am." The authoritarian approach says, "I dominate, therefore I am," whereas ConnectAbility can be illustrated by declaring, "I relate, therefore I am." ConnectAbility involves respect for others, enhanced by finding the similarities with them, not the differences.

François-Marie Arouet, better known as Voltaire, is famous for his social and political satire aimed at ridiculing the vanity of kings and clerics. Arguably France's greatest dramatist of the 18th century, Voltaire was, according to present-day pundits in an article in *The Wall Street Journal*, "unsparing in his criticism of the foibles of clerics . . . regularly decrying what he called

Customer Copy

Ben Franklin Institute
PO Box 7128
Cave Creek, AZ 85327
(800) 643-0797

* *

Date: 03-OCT-2013
Time: 09:46:36 AM
Card Type: Visa
Card Number: XXXX1697
Trans ID: 5585409806
Auth Code: 09097D
Approved Amt: $21.55

* *
I AGREE TO PAY THE ABOVE TOTAL
ACCORDING TO MY CARD ISSUER
AGREEMENT.

L'Infame, the 'infamy' of superstition, fanaticism and intolerance." Clearly, Voltaire set the pace of ConnectAbility for years and centuries to come by facing social reality so bravely at a time when politics were not bound by rule of law. Only by his own wit and social charm was Voltaire able to write so truthfully about the "infamous" society around him and get away with it.

Minding Your Business

Have you ever wondered why so many of the stories you hear about investments in the stock market are sad ones? Status-based thinking may give us a clue. Most stories seem to be about significant losses rather than gains, unless the individual is an expert investor and focuses on that activity as a life priority. It turns out smart investing involves not only when to buy, but equally important, when to sell. Most amateurs buy and then forget about that particular stock—until they need to take the money out for some reason or other, totally unconnected to the stock's performance.

Why is it so hard for us to sell a stock we've owned for a while? If it's doing well, then we're inclined to keep it, as it feels successful. If it has dropped in value, then we have to wait till it regains its "true" value. If it hasn't done anything—up or down—then we wait to see which direction it'll take. No matter what its activity, we find no reason to sell. That's stock market investing, Status Factor style. Stay with the status quo, no matter what's happening around us.

So what is ConnectAbility investing? Just like staying aware of others' perspectives in business interaction, Awareness Factor investing means staying aware of the marketplace information on your stock on a moment-to-moment (or at least week-to-week) basis. Just as there's a time to buy, there's a time to sell. This type of investing takes more time and effort, but it's much more profitable.

Also, we tend to be more attracted to high-risk investments than to sensible, conservative ones. According to the *Consumer Reports Money Adviser*, "Our brains experience greater pleasure (via a surge of dopamine) at the prospect of making money when there are high risks involved than when it's a sure thing. The reason is that the dopamine rush corresponds with the anticipation of making money, not actually getting it." Emotions often get in the way when it's time to sell as well. It's still hard for me to sell a stock that has dropped in value, even when I'm aware of the timely changes in the marketplace. There's something about my brain that hates to sell at a loss—a kind of built-in Status Factor. Neuroscientists have a name for this—"loss aversion."

At New York University's Center for Brain Imaging, individuals are given MRI scans and at the same time asked to choose between two investment options—a no-loss situation or gambling to win X or lose Y. A decision must then be made within three seconds. For one group of choices, the subjects were instructed to make their decisions as if they were building a stock portfolio, that is, building on the premise that some losses could be overcome by other gains. The importance of this research is that people hate to lose once they've made their investment, as the MRI scans reveal that loss is interpreted by the human brain as weakness (i.e., we end up with a status-based, stick-with-what-you-have decision). Selling at a loss brings on some anxiety, triggering activity in the amygdala, which in turn overwhelms the rational, thinking prefrontal cortex, resulting in the inability to make a logically processed decision. The fear of weakness, in other words, overshadows the logical decision-making process to get out of a bad deal.[2]

Sell with Assurance/Lead with Trust

There are two main points to take away from this research because of what we've learned about how the brain functions, two sensible principles in which we can have more confidence: (1) people tend to reject risky propositions (unless they're seduced by the possibility of great gains with little investment with a rationale for coming out ahead, minimizing the sense of risk), and (2) those who are less fearful might turn out to be better decision makers. The ramifications of the first point are many. For one, sales efforts may become more successful if the purchaser perceives less risk involved. That means taking some of the mystery out of the process and, instead, connecting as many dots as possible for the customer or client—taking him or her from status-based fear to awareness-based openness. Questions such as, "What is the useful life of this product?" "How does the product/service work?" "Whom do I call if I have questions?" need to be answered.

Another ramification: the trust built up in awareness-type selling is crucial to resolving some of the anxiety that comes up in dealing with *new* services or products. In other words, awareness-based selling is validated by this research. Both of these points can be consolidated by selling that connects the dots for the customer in the context of an awareness-based, trust-building relationship.

The second point highlights the fact that those who are less fearful make better decisions because they can look more objectively at risk-laden opportunities. Less fear or anxiety means a less reactive amygdala and a more efficient judgment-making prefrontal cortex. So it's better to have leaders (as well as salespeople) who create a context of trust and confidence. Leaders who take the ConnectAbility approach and build trust and openness will have top-level executives making better decisions, and so on down the line of midlevel executives and managers—all making better decisions because there is less fear in the organization's culture.

From Blind Optimism to Brutal Reality

Returning to our original focus on the Status Factor, it must be said that there are many who feel drawn to it.

Certainly, the hierarchical structure of the Status Factor has the ring of virtue and morality to it. We *ought* to obey the rules of the hierarchy, do what's "right," to follow the letter of the law. In the abstract, there is no fault with this. But where does the truth lie, with awareness or status? Is either more virtuous than the other?

In the incident described in Chapter 2, weapons *should* be removed from organizations. That's the abstraction that the lieutenant followed when he decided to take the AK rifle from the monastery. He was following his orders, to the letter. With hierarchy-based status, there's no thinking necessary—simplicity reigns. However, with awareness, complexity reigns. There is no monopoly on truth; categorizing others simplistically doesn't help awareness.

An individual who gives priority to the brutal reality of existing business challenges is obviously more effective with his or her associates than the hierarchy-based counterpart who may prefer blind optimism. A leader who makes others feel heard and understood—and thereby less defensive—is much more likely to motivate others. As a result, he or she is apt to be much more successful when it comes to the bottom line of generating profits. But getting from one to the other is no easy task.

So how does one get from one to the other? What are the essential and concrete differences between the two ways of thinking? Is there a way of understanding the differences in terms of human values? We'll answer all these questions in the next chapter.

CHAPTER 4

Men, Women, and Faking It

KEY 4: EXPRESS WHAT IS RELEVANT AND TRUE FOR YOU

In developing strong partnerships with your colleagues and customers, understand that being honest is not about "letting it all hang out." Rather, it's expressing what is true for you and relevant to the situation at hand, while being mindful of the audience receiving the information. Honesty is a skill, as much as it is a component of one's character.

IS THERE A possible gender bias in ConnectAbility? It's often said that women are better listeners than men. Are men who are comfortable with the Awareness Factor also more comfortable with their "feminine" side, such as intuition and emotional sensitivity? Are women effective in business more in touch with their "masculine" side, such as logic and objectivity?

Even the most powerful men in the military have room for their intuitive, supportive side. Colin Powell, for example, prior to his stint as secretary of state, was the highest-ranking officer in the U.S. armed forces. Under

President Reagan, he accepted the position of chief of Forces Command (FORSCOM), responsible for more than one million U.S. troops, yet he allowed himself sufficient emotional sensitivity to be a listening post for those serving under his command. Powell states in his book, *My American Journey*, that "leadership is problem solving. The day soldiers stop bringing you their problems is the day you have stopped leading them. They have either lost confidence that you can help them or concluded that you do not care. Either case is a failure of leadership." After serving in the Army for 35 years, Powell went on to assist the president on national security affairs and then became the 12th chairman of the Joint Chiefs of Staff before becoming secretary of state. He was a great leader, by any measure. The Awareness Factor of listening to others was primary for him. He wasn't afraid to let emotions come into play.

What this says to those of us in the workplace is that as we become more mature as professionals and leaders, we allow the qualities of the opposite gender to emerge within us. So men, using their ConnectAbility at work, may allow their emotions to play a larger function in their decision making, particularly when it comes to making judgments about others in the workplace. They may allow their intuition or gut feelings to play a larger role as they decide whom to trust with greater responsibility, whom to assign to tough jobs, and with whom to align in the process of collective leadership.

Women who succeed in business, on the other hand, are often helped by their confidence in their own decision making as they begin to feel more comfortable making crucial decisions based on logic and facts rather than solely on feelings and shared opinion. "You need to be . . . willing to make statements affirmatively and take ownership of your ideas," says Julie Hembrock Daum, practice leader of Spencer Stuart, in an issue of *Newsweek*. Yet, despite the fact that more than half of all managers and professionals are female, just 2 percent of Fortune 1000 CEOs and only 7.9 percent of Fortune 500 top earners are women. What's the problem?

Part of the problem may be that many women are reluctant to give up their best child-rearing years to devote the long hours and globe-circling travel that seem to make up the hoops we must jump through to achieve top leadership status. In fact, this may be a primary reason since countless surveys reveal that male and female leadership styles show few differences, according to an analysis by the New York–based Catalyst research group. A bigger problem may be that women see themselves as stereotypes more than is justified by the facts. The Catalyst group surveyed 296 leaders of both genders about leadership effectiveness. Men gave women high marks for supportive and rewarding skills, but gave themselves more credit for four critical leadership skills—problem solving, inspiring, delegating, and influencing upward (having impact on those above you). So this male prejudice may, in part, account for women's small ranks at the highest levels of leadership.

Women, in agreement with men for the most part, gave men more credit for networking, influencing upward, and delegating. "These are the perceptions, not the reality," says Catalyst President Ilene Lang in an article in *The Wall Street Journal*. "Women as well as men perceive women leaders as better at caretaker behaviors and men as better at take-charge behaviors. . . . Men aren't expected to be supportive." Yet Powell, one of the most effective leaders, shows just how support can be an important part of a man's leadership style.[1]

What Men and Women Have to Offer One Another

The bottom line is that both genders, as they learn to tap their deeper selves in the workplace, are strengthened by allowing those qualities—initially

Good leaders transcend gender roles. The common perception is that, as leaders, women are better caretakers and men are better at taking charge. The truth is that the best leaders, men or women, are good at both.

thought of as opposite to their gender identity—to emerge with growing confidence. The woman who ends up in a top executive role often surprises the business community with her masculine leadership style. But a closer look reveals that the success is due not to adopting a masculine style but rather to amalgamating the best of the feminine and masculine within her. The well-balanced female leader can think as logically as any man but has not forsaken her intuition and emotional sensibilities.

Despite this, many women feel betrayed by corporate America, enough to be suing—and winning. Boeing settled one suit brought by female employees charging gender discrimination for $72.5 million. Morgan Stanley settled a similar suit for $54 million. All this because the Civil Rights Act of 1991 allows for substantial punitive damages against companies discriminating by gender. Such suits help get the worst offenders back in line. There is no place for sexual discrimination in today's workplace. Successful women are proving adept at taking charge, and their male counterparts are showing their feelings can come into play as well.

Jane Goodall, founder of the Jane Goodall Institute for Wildlife Research and wildlife preservation spokeswoman, is an excellent example of a combination of female sensibilities and male intellectual independence. "With language we can ask, as no other living being, those questions about who we are and why we are here," she claimed. "And this highly developed intellect means, surely, that we have a responsibility toward other life-forms of our planet." Ms. Goodall had the emotional sensitivity to the subhuman primates with whom she worked but also the independent intellect to communicate her philosophy as a lone voice for a neglected cause.

As the technology of electronic networking makes the use of our "highly developed intellect" even more important, the role of women becomes more integrated into the business realm. According to Sheryl Sandberg, COO of the online networking site Facebook, "Facebook allows people to be their authentic selves online and therefore use the power of technology to discover each other and share who they really are." ConnectAbility, with its focus on authentic expression and understanding of others at a deeper level (Awareness of Others), is well served by electronic networking and offers a platform for women to share and communicate at an equal level. Using language that allows us to communicate our authentic selves (presentation skills), whether in person or electronically, levels the playing field. Women no longer need to find themselves forced into subservient roles, merely echoing their male counterparts' decisions. Women are now able to shed their stereotypic role of followers and share leadership equally with men.[2]

By the same token, men who succeed in the 21st century are often able to transcend the male macho role of playing by the rules only and obfuscating any emotion as distraction. Instead they allow their emotional awareness of interpersonal dynamics to improve their chances of surviving in a terribly complex world of corporate management. A concern for ethics, for example, was deemed more feminine in years past; today that is no longer the case. Oliver Stone's classic 1987 film, *Wall Street*—starring Michael Douglas as corporate raider Gordon Gekko who utters the infamous line, "Greed, for lack of a better term, is good"—demonstrates the harsh consequences for unethical behavior: jail time.

Tips for Advancing Your ConnectAbility

- **Men with ConnectAbility are not afraid to go with their gut feelings** when making decisions about people.
- Men and women continue to stereotype one another's contributions along gender lines. **Those with ConnectAbility transcend gender stereotypes.**
- **Women with ConnectAbility have had to fight for the respect they deserve** as they consolidate the best of male and female leadership skills. Understanding and accepting strong women leaders is a step forward in this ongoing challenge.

In the next section we'll explore how a "feel-good" hormone, oxytocin, can enhance the level of trust in both men and women. By engaging our Awareness of Influence, we can initiate business transactions more effectively, triggering the "trust" hormone.

The Biochemistry of Trust

Being your authentic self as an awareness-based model of our times, whether man or woman, involves openness to this crossover phenomenon in which both genders act more similarly than ever before. Men can be more open to their emotional sensibilities and women can be more assertive and open to their urges for powerful leadership positions. This puts men on an equal footing when it comes to understanding the causes of motivation, and puts women on an equal footing when it comes to choosing the best assignments for those under their leadership.

At the biochemical level, male-oriented testosterone (actually, dihy-drotestosterone—DHT) is, as we all know, associated with male aggression. In a study done in Zurich, Switzerland, researchers found that men do indeed experience a rise in DHT when feeling distrusting and angry, while women don't. Interestingly, though, when either men or women become more trusting, their level of oxytocin increases. Dr. Paul Zac and his colleagues in Zurich, when they administered oxytocin to 29 out of 178 volunteers by nasal spray, found that both men and women became more trusting in a money negotiation transaction than those who did not receive the spray.[3]

So what do we learn from this? For one thing, it is more beneficial to engage a sense of trust rather than competitiveness or belligerence if we're looking for successful negotiations and sales transactions; approaching with antagonism will only trigger a release of DHT in men. Leading with trust, on the other hand, may release more oxytocin, and therefore a greater sense of comfort and cooperation, in both sexes. Conveying trustworthiness is the best approach for success—whether in sales, negotiations, or any other aspect of business.

Understanding of Others' Emotions Grows with Maturity

Understanding the dynamics of male and female emotions is something we learn as children. From age five onward, we are constantly creating theories as to why certain people feel what they feel. We look at the circumstances preceding a particular emotional expression and create a causal relationship between the two. "Johnny called me names because he doesn't like me," says five-year-old Peggy, cute as a button. As adults, we may have a different theory—Johnny adores Peggy but doesn't have the skills to get her attention any other way.

Similarly, as adults, our first theory as to why someone has a certain emotional reaction may be wrong. What does help us to be more accurate is the experience of time and the accumulation of emotional awareness, involving refined empathy and an understanding of how we felt under similar circumstances. Our ability to link emotions to their antecedents is fully functioning at about age five, but the accuracy grows only with time and experience. We become increasingly aware of why people have certain feelings and how each person's personality fits into the overall picture of emotional reaction. Each one of us is unique, particularly when it comes to emotional personalities. But how do we acquire our own unique emotional makeup? Certainly, a part of it is genetic inheritance from our parents. What about the rest?

Tips for Advancing Your ConnectAbility

- **Trust**, an important component of successful business, is easier for women than men but essential for both if they are going to succeed.
- Leading with a competitive edge just invites the other to adrenaline-driven defensiveness. **Leading with trust** invites open-minded acceptance; the risk is worth taking.
- **ConnectAbility grows with experience.** Keep an open mind to differences in people.

The Baby Steps of Learning ConnectAbility

The first step in how ConnectAbility develops in children is the ability to discern different emotions on parents' faces. Ever watch a mother and infant interact as they exchange baby talk with one another? They appear to be inextricably linked. The infant responds with a smile to the parent's smile, or with a look of surprise or even a frown to a similar expression on the part of the parent. This is definitely communication. The infant is learning the first step—noticing—in the very complex process of emotional communication. In fact, the infant is learning two modes of noticing—facial expression and voice.

The next stage, of course, increases in complexity. This second stage—usually learned between the ages of two and four and a half—involves three steps: the ability to (1) label emotions or at least be aware of feeling them, (2) distinguish situations that will lead to emotional reactions, and (3) understand why certain situations lead to certain emotions and the consequences of expressing these emotions.

The first categories of emotions that are recognized, of course, are good or happy and bad or sad. It's like learning the primary colors of red, blue, and yellow before learning the myriad combinations thereof. Once good emotions can be distinguished from bad, all their variations—bad leading to anger, jealousy, bitterness, and so forth and good leading to love, pleasure, contentment, and so on—can also be identified.

The next stage involves the awareness that others' emotions can be different from one's own and that it may be possible to understand others' emotions by getting personal information about them.

The final stage for children learning about ConnectAbility involves four steps: (1) learning that others may hide their emotions, and that families and cultures have certain rules about which emotions are acceptable to share and which aren't; (2) learning how to share one's own emotions without showing extremes; (3) discovering that it's possible to have two or more emotions at the same time that actually conflict with one another; and (4) finding out that emotions are very complex and almost impossible to understand completely.

Children learn all this in the same order for the most part but at very different rates. Those who feel secure and nurtured probably learn most quickly

> **When in doubt, take your time.** Even children learn that it's possible to have two conflicting emotions at the same time. That's OK—don't try to resolve such conflict immediately. It takes time.

while those who are not nurtured or are abused or neglected will learn much more slowly as their task of emotional survival may take almost all their emotional resources, leaving little for the learning process. They learn, of course, but what they learn is how to defend themselves from very painful emotions brought about by their unsavory environment. They have little time left for learning about their feelings or others' feelings when they feel threatened or insecure from day to day.

How We Learn the Skills of ConnectAbility

Before the age of five or six, most children are fairly spontaneous with their emotions. Raised in a stable environment, they share their feelings somewhat freely, especially with one another and sometimes even with their parents and their parents' friends. Think of the main comedic thrust of the old cartoon character Dennis the Menace, who would repeat what he heard his parents say about their guests after the guests' arrival, to the embarrassment of all. When this same feature of brash openness is seen in adults, we call it immaturity or naïveté. If they do it in public with extreme elegance and deftness, we call them comedians, sharing what we all know to be true but dare not say in public. Dissembling (concealing feelings or intentions) is not learned until a few years later.

So being our authentic self in the workplace involves having gone through the school of hard knocks in terms of making the mistakes of emotional miscommunication until we get it right. Having learned to dissemble our emotions, that is, to hide what we think is unacceptable, untoward, or even dangerous to our career tracks, we're now exploring a reversal of that process to share more openly to reveal our authentic self.

It's like so many other things—we must learn something well before we learn to do what we don't usually do. If we're going to share how we really feel about taboo topics in front of a captive audience, we must learn the art of comedy—how to be to the point, to be dramatically effective, and to share those things that others tend to sweep under the rug—without offending too much. How much we offend depends on the brand of humor.

You wouldn't expect to do trick riding on a horse unless you mastered the basic skills of horse riding and had them down pat. You wouldn't dare fly planes as "recklessly" as the Blue Angels until you learned how to fly straight. In other words, you can be your authentic self in the workplace only after you've learned to understand and control your feelings impeccably. Being your real self at work doesn't mean letting it all hang out. On the contrary, it means having the emotional awareness to identify your ongoing feelings and the mindfulness to be sensitive as to how others may react to your sharing. What that does is enable you to share your feelings with integrity. You share your real self after due consideration of what your true self consists of in some particular situation. And you do so mindful of the consequences of your sharing. It's the integrity that keeps you honest about the process.

Man/Woman Relationships

Most agree that ongoing relationships between men and women, such as marriage, are hard work. That work is all about negotiation—my radio station or

Be open, but keep your audience in mind. Awareness sharing involves openness with a concern for its effect on the listener. That's where the integrity comes in—to be true to yourself while taking into consideration how your audience is affected by what you share. There's a sense of appropriateness and timing that make such openness acceptable.

yours in the car, which restaurant to go to, or which movie, or when to go to bed. Left alone without another, there would be no need to negotiate, but we choose to share our living space with a partner and that needs negotiation, for small items as much as big ones.

When men and women work together, the dynamics can be similar to those of a marriage—that is to say, their respective attitudes toward emotions may be similar. Men and women may see things differently at work. He is more interested in solving problems. She wants problems solved as well but may take a more emotionally open response to the challenge at hand.

One of the greatest battles between two people in a relationship may be the degree to which emotions are expressed, if at all. Often, women need more emotional validation while men tend to say, "What, me worry about feelings? I've got problems to solve, including the ones you create by demanding that I get all emotional about nothing important."

Women, particularly as they mature in a marriage, often crave more power than they accepted at the beginning of the relationship. Carl Jung was well aware of this. He referred to the deeper soul of women as Animus—the hidden male counterpart of her personality—and the deeper soul of men as Anima—the hidden female counterpart of his personality. According to Jung, women, as they mature, crave more power to assert their deeper selves in a more forceful manner, while men, as they mature, may allow their more feminine side to emerge as they relax into their emotional selves, becoming more open to their vulnerabilities and needs for relationship. These dynamics reveal themselves in the workplace as well, as women become more assertive with business experience and a number of men feel more comfortable with their emotions as they gain more leadership responsibility.

Learning the "Cool" Skills of Group Affiliation

Developing the authentic qualities inherent in ConnectAbility involves overcoming the dissembling style of early teenage years. For some this style

Tips for Advancing Your ConnectAbility

- **Remember: all human emotions are made up of either good feelings or bad feelings.** That's the starting point of the Awareness Factor.
- **Honesty is not "letting it all hang out."** It's expressing what is *true* and *relevant* to the situation, and being *mindful* of the party to whom the communication is directed. Without mindfulness you have narcissism. Honesty is a skill, as much as it is a component of one's character.
- **As they mature, men and women begin to take on each other's characteristics.** Men become more open to emotions, women to becoming more assertive. Those with ConnectAbility invite and accept this transformation.

extends into adulthood. As early as age three, we can begin to understand the consequences of our emotions. When something forbidden is done, we fear the subsequent punishment. When we yell in a quiet room, we fear rebuke. When we fear the bogeyman in the closet, we know running to our parents will assuage that emotion.

One of the biggest leaps in terms of emotional sensitivity comes when we begin to find friendship in alliances. It's one thing to make it work with one other, yet it's quite another to make a group friendship work. Here we begin to focus on becoming acceptable to the group and avoiding being rejected for being insensitive to the group norms. That's precisely why adolescents become so enmeshed in their socializing. By that time, a couple of friends give way to small groups in terms of "best" friends. Not that these friends disappear, but the clique becomes paramount.

The norms of such cliques are much more complex and finely tuned than appears on the surface. Here's where we first learn to fake our real feelings and to appear cool and unflappable. This is not a time for authentic intimacy but rather for feigned confidence despite the pervasive insecurities characterized by that age.

No wonder there are so many qualifiers in early teens' language. Dissembling, or putting on a false emotional front, appears to be what succeeds among these children becoming adults. They've reached the age when spontaneous emotions aren't seen as "cool." In time, they will hopefully learn to balance controlled emotions with a certain openness to authenticity—but not quite yet. Their long conversations with confidants reveal how important group acceptance is to them as they weigh and judge the actions of others.

It's at this stage of emotional development that attempts at understanding others' personalities in parsing their emotional decisions is so important. Teenagers begin to discuss these social dynamics with some greater precision, replacing *good* and *bad* as descriptors of emotion with terms such as *pride*, *guilt*, and *jealousy*.

Dissembling: The Art of Hiding Your Feelings

Being your real self in the workplace with ConnectAbility does not mean blatant spontaneity. Most important is the sense of appropriateness and timing that makes such openness acceptable. It involves, first of all, keeping close track of how you're feeling from moment to moment, and only then sharing your feelings in the context that can benefit from such sharing. There is indeed a fine line between dissembling your emotions to fit into the context on the one hand, and having the courage to share what you truly feel even though it may not find instant understanding and acceptance. If your intent is to be of service to others, then the intimate sharing of what may not immediately find acceptance will, in the long run, stand you in good stead, as the judgment you reveal becomes respected over time.

The skill of gaining control over total emotional spontaneity grows over the span of the elementary school years. By adolescence, this skill is finely tuned. Social acceptance is so critical at this stage that emotional dissembling becomes the modus operandi of social success. Children who fail at this social skill may end up friendless and marginalized. If Nancy fails to curb her short temper and bossy demands, she may be ostracized by her peers. If Peter cowers at the prospect of confronting those who tease or harass him, he may lose face in his group and be seen as an outsider.

In the adult world, dissembling still plays a significant role. One doesn't just mouth off to an aggressive boss. Nor does the boss casually mouth off to a lazy employee. In the workplace, dissembling such emotions as anger and anxiety is essential. But when the more moderate emotions are also hidden, then the question of degree comes into play: how much dissembling and how much authentic emotion is required to build a strong connection?

To Fake or Be Your Real Self

Jack's boss, Nicole, is rude bordering on abusive. Nicole is an excellent executive in the sense that she oversees many functions and keeps all the brush fires doused. But this means that she's always under stress. She doesn't suffer fools gladly and is fairly outspoken about her dissatisfactions. She truly appreciates Jack, her administrative assistant, and this is easily seen by the fact that she yells at him much less frequently than at others and with a rare gentility.

Tips for Advancing Your ConnectAbility

- **The urge to belong starts early in life** and remains a very strong need throughout. This helps us understand the power of "groupthink."
- **Equally strong is the urge to feel understood.** This also begins in childhood and remains a strong need throughout life.
- **The challenge of authenticity**, how honest to be in any particular setting, continues through life as well. Those who take greater risks with honesty and are skilled at it have the potential to become respected leaders.

However, she does have a tendency to come across as nasty to Jack, and he is quite sensitive to conflict and feels stressed by Nicole's outbursts. What should Jack do?

One option is to share with Nicole that stress is an outcome of her intense personality and to find ways to diminish this stress. If Nicole is open to some change, she might encourage Jack to "talk back" to her, not in an aggressive fashion but in a teasing mode, so that when Nicole yells one of her frequent demands, Jack would have the permission to yell back, to the small extent he might muster, in a joking mode. If Nicole understands Jack's dilemma and can go with the flow in terms of hearing her own intensity come back at her in a small way, then Jack might feel less stress. Just saying the words in an uncharacteristic mode may release the tension otherwise building up within him.

The ability to release stress by acknowledging its presence to a boss who causes it is one example of releasing the real self. The outcome in this case is a more comfortable relationship with a boss who, other than her emotional intensity, is great to work for. By being able to return that intensity in some small way, Jack becomes a more comfortable and productive individual who is a better resource for his boss.

Generally, we want to feel more comfortable at work. We could fake it when we're not feeling that great or we could reveal some of what might be causing the stress. The result is the likelihood of feeling better. Stress and anger are two emotions that make us feel bad. Whatever resources we can use to open up and reveal that we're uncomfortable and then find options to relieve these emotions will only bring more satisfaction to the job.

Some Things You Just Can't Fake—Like a Simple Smile

Often we think we're quite successful at dissembling when the truth is that we're not fooling anybody. Paul Ekman, the world's foremost expert on emotional expression and author of 14 books, including *Emotions Revealed*, maintains that some emotions are almost impossible to fake. A genuine smile, for example, involves not only the zygomatic major muscles to create the smiling mouth but also the pars orbitalis, which circles the eyes. A fake smile most

Tips for Advancing Your ConnectAbility

- **Reacting with some intensity** in response to an intense individual can relieve some of the stress in an otherwise uncomfortable situation, as long as it's done with no hostility and a touch of humor.
- **Acknowledging discomfort** when it occurs, if done appropriately, can relieve much of that discomfort.
- **Setting limits** in situations causing discomfort and even abuse garners respect.

often reveals itself by not involving those eye muscles. And those eye muscles will not easily obey the will. In other words, a genuine smile comes from the heart, not the brain. If you try to smile while not being your true self in the moment, others will know it. "Unlike body language," Canadian researcher Stephen Porter told *The Week* in May 2008, "you can't monitor or completely control what's going on in your face." In short, phonies who try to please by smiling are not fooling those around them.

Malcolm Gladwell, in his book *Blink*, describes this ability to see the true emotions despite attempts at dissembling. We do it so automatically and unconsciously that we feel as though we're reading others' minds. Actually, writes Gladwell, "there is enough accessible information in a face to make everyday mind reading possible. When someone tells us 'I love you,' we look immediately and directly at him or her because by looking at the face, we can know . . . about whether the sentiment is genuine."

Through their research, psychologists Mark Frank and Paul Ekman were able to isolate 46 facial movements and code them into more than 10,000 microexpressions in what they call the Facial Action Coding System. This system has proven to detect lying with an accuracy of 76 percent. Brain scientists have even figured out what parts of the brain become activated when people lie. Those who are trained to interpret these microexpressions by the Transportation Security Administration are known as behavioral detection officers. Companies such as No Lie MRI of San Diego and Cephos of Pepperell, Massachusetts, are looking to use brain-scan technology for airport and other security challenges.[4] Lying about our emotions, especially where such technology exists, becomes more and more of a challenge.

By being your real self in the workplace, you don't have to worry about dissembling. The more you can share how you really feel—appropriately, of course—the more genuine you come across. Not all of us are equal when it comes to reading others' emotions. How good we are has a lot to do with our early experience, as mentioned earlier. Even as children, some of us are more expert at reading others' emotions. Those who are better at it are more liked by their peers and teachers. And they also tend to treat others better as well. So the skills involved in the Awareness Factor are self-reinforcing.

In Sum

Successful men and women in the workplace are more alike than different when it comes to dealing with emotions, even though common wisdom characterizes women as caretakers and men as problem solvers. Well-known leaders such as Colin Powell and Jane Goodall prove this common wisdom wrong.

We learn as children how to differentiate emotions and how to keep our expressions in check. As teenagers we learn how to dissemble and appear cool. With maturity we have the opportunity to regain a sense of our deeper honesty but now tempered by our awareness of how we affect others with our honesty.

As values about gender expression evolve in our culture, women who were once ready to settle for submissive roles are now determined to claim equality and their full share of respect, both at home and at work. Some organiza-

Don't even try to fake a smile. You can't fake a genuine smile, so don't try it. Instead, let the smile come from your feeling of judgment-free awareness and genuine support.

tions have to be reminded of this in a court of law. And it's still true that male executives are more readily recognized for their success than are women executives, even when their levels of competency are equal.

And finally, faking emotions doesn't wear well over time. A simple smile can't be faked. The better course is to feel the smile from a genuine value system of nonjudgmental awareness.

In the next chapter, we'll see how reframing negative events into more bearable, positive ones can help. Emotions sometimes rule, but reframing allows us to broaden and build. We'll also see how bad emotions can be signposts to help guide us to our next move, if we handle them with awareness.

Tips for Advancing Your ConnectAbility

- **Honesty begins with a smile**—an honest one.
- **Just be real.** Facial expressions make it difficult to lie.
- **Learning how to read others' faces more accurately** results in others finding you more acceptable and trustworthy. The Awareness Factor pays off.

CHAPTER 5

Becoming Agile in Business Relationships

KEY 5: ENGAGE YOUR AUDIENCE WITH HUMOR

In developing strong partnerships with your colleagues and customers, laughter, in response to appropriate humor, can be the shortest path between you and them, whether that party is one or an audience of hundreds. In an authentic, supportive context, laughter improves overall communication and may help bottom-line results.

IT'S BEEN A full day—meetings, returning important phone calls, a long dinner with a valuable prospect—and you're burning the midnight oil, trying to meet a grueling deadline. But you're not alone; there are others working after hours as well. You hear laughter in the hallway—a woman giggling, followed by a couple of men laughing openly in response—and you can't help but feel left out, mildly annoyed, or just plain curious. There is a contagion in the air when spontaneous emotions burst forth. Many within earshot feel the need to know what it's about, even if they feign disinterest. The truth is that we're all drawn to the drama of fully expressed emotions. What is it that makes emotional expression so powerful? Shouldn't reason master emotion? Shouldn't we be controlling our emotional impulse to communicate our feelings?

In addition to the ability to perceive and appraise emotions accurately, according to the founders of the concept of emotional intelligence, EI also involves using emotions to clarify thinking, communicating emotions better, and managing emotions in oneself and others—which brings us back to the power of laughter as an emotional form of communication. Certainly, good communication skills go a long way to revealing underlying emotions. But the most emotionally revealing sounds we hear from others come in a non-verbal form of oral communication—laughter.

Let's take a look at the phenomenon of laughter as an example of how emotions can be communicated effectively without words. From a technical point of view, laughter is characterized by a sharp, sudden onset and high-pitched vocalization, and sometimes high volume. There is one more feature common to this type of vocalization that can be referred to as technical: amplitude modulation, meaning a wide range of pitch, from low to high, characteristic of laughter.

To understand the emotional aspects of laughter, let's consider the various effects it has on us. First of all, there is a great difference among individuals in terms of how they respond to these emotional signals. The most important factor is the relationship between the sender of such signals and the receiver. Is the laughter coming from a friend or an enemy? Laughter is often at someone's expense.

We're Born with ConnectAbility

As it turns out, even infants have the ability to read other infants' crying. "People have always known that babies cry when they hear other babies cry,"

A joke a day . . . Want to make better connections? Humor resulting in laughter is a great way to connect emotionally with an audience of one or many.

states psychologist Martin Hoffman of New York University in a *Newsweek* article. An Italian study explored whether this contagious crying was due to annoyance or empathy. When recordings of other babies' crying were played, the infants cried, but not when they heard recordings of their own crying. The result, according to Dr. Hoffman: "There is some rudimentary empathy in place, right from birth." Apparently, responding to another person's crying with empathy begins very early in life.

If the laugher is emotionally connected to you, you will likely feel even closer. Referred to as "empathic resonance" by Daniel Goleman and "emotional contagion" by others, some researchers have found that two individuals sharing a good laugh begin to synchronize their expressions, postures, and emotions. "Indeed," says Goleman in an issue of *Psychotherapy Networker*, "laughter may be the shortest distance between two brains, an unstoppable infectious spread that builds an instant social bond."

Those with ConnectAbility are much more likely to respond to laughter in a flexible, productive manner. Hearing laughter from someone you feel close to can lead to creative efforts or affection or serious problem solving at an intimate level, depending on the situation. It's the flexibility to respond appropriately—adaptability or agility skills—that makes you emotionally aware. As a result, the importance of sharing laughter in sales, leadership, teamwork, and negotiation becomes apparent.

There is also a great distinction between sensitive hearers and nonsensitive ones. The most blatant example of this is how parents react to infant cries of distress. Many parents, for example, are able to distinguish among various cries, such as those expressing pain, hunger, or wet diapers. Those parents with histories of abuse and neglect in their own lives appear to be unable to distinguish among the different types of crying, and instead react to all cries as annoying and noxious.

This leads to a very interesting question: Are parents who abuse children deficient in their perceptive abilities, or do they just lack ConnectAbility? The scientific finding that abusive parents react to crying with higher cardiac and electro-dermal responses (indications of higher emotional arousal) just compounds the question. It may be that abusive parents are unable to help themselves because their own emotional responses to their infants are so intense while at the same time they are insensitive to the finer nuances, which are blocked out by their own intensity.

Are there some people just too injured by childhood abuse to be sensitive to what matters in the workplace? Does that give you a different perspective of those you considered insensitive to your needs at work?

The Team That Laughs Together . . .

When it comes to laughter, it appears that what is important is the social context in which it occurs. Therefore, what is said prior to laughter determines its effect more than any other single variable. In terms of social context, what matters is the sex of the individuals involved and whether they're friends or strangers. The laugh of a female who approaches a male who is a stranger will most likely have sexual overtones. A female's laugh in a mixed group such as a business cocktail party will likely have flirtatious overtones. That exact same laughter, as heard by a nearby female, may result in an aggressive or withdrawal reaction that we might characterize as jealousy or competitiveness.

In a business setting, the dynamics of a gathering of people, small or large, are even more influential in determining the effects of laughter. Is the boss in the group or within hearing range? Are there political dynamics inherent in the group involving competition or strategizing? Perhaps that's why laughter isn't that common among business groups, unless the leader initiates the appropriate context. The mark of an effective motivational speaker is his or her ability to get the audience laughing. Then they are more likely to be all on the same wavelength, and the speaker has a better chance of influencing the audience.

Coming from the perspective of ConnectAbility and facing the emotional states in yourself and others in the moments you share means that your laugh-

It's all about the timing. Authentic communication followed by laughter (in response to a good joke or witty remark) can bring about a harmonious connection between speaker and audience.

Tips for Advancing Your ConnectAbility

- **Laughter is a special form of communication**, very different from speech. Master an understanding of its dynamics and you increase your ConnectAbility.
- **Laughter, from appropriate humor**, can form the shortest distance between two minds.
- **Laughter, in an authentic, supportive context**, improves overall communication and may help bottom-line productivity.

ter is in a sensitive context of people with whom you have a connection. The authenticity you express will have the effect of making your laughter more connective with others. To the extent that one of the effects of laughter is to bring others into a synchrony of emotion (when it's preceded by authentic communication), you and your associates will share a closer sense of community when you laugh together, and this can bring a greater sense of joy and meaning to work.

Reading the Faces of Business

Would you be better off if you could accurately read the faces of your customers, clients, even bosses and associates? The answer is obvious. The more easily you can read others' emotions, the more comfortable you'll be with your own authentic feelings. Reading others' faces more accurately allows you to gauge what feelings are appropriate to share in any given setting, whether it involves selling, managing others, or working as a team. Remember, ConnectAbility is not being authentic with your feelings *regardless* of the context. Rather, it is being sensitive to the context and then choosing how to share your authentic feelings *sensibly and appropriately*. That fine distinction makes all the difference.

Let's look at some research on emotional communication. Charles Darwin focused on two basic emotions when he studied animals across the board—smiling approval and frowning disapproval. More recently, scientists have come up with about a half-dozen basic emotions: happiness, sadness, anger, fear, disgust, and surprise. Some emotions, such as a smile indicating happiness, can be and often is faked in the effort to provide a social lubricant when things get tense, or even as a polite demeanor in the absence of any true emotion. Paul Ekman, guru of emotional recognition, has been able to distinguish between the two. In the false smile, the eye areas are not engaged; the smile is less symmetrical and may disappear suddenly. But many of us—at least those without ConnectAbility—may miss the difference since it is so subtle in appearance.

ConnectAbility helps us distinguish between the authentic and the faked smile. How? By being more in touch with our feelings on a moment-to-moment basis. Aware of our gut feelings, we can "feel" that the faked smile is what it is—inauthentic. A fake smile only works for those who are not in touch with their feelings. The "faker" may think he's getting away with something.

Anyone with access to the workings of the brain, however, would see a significant difference. When deception takes place, different parts of the brain are activated. Lying is an effortful process involving much activity in the thinking prefrontal cortex but also emotional activity in the limbic system, much more so than someone being truthful about something, who doesn't have to work so hard at keeping in mind two sets of data—the truth and the lie. When lying takes place, says Scott H. Faro, director of Temple University's Functional Brain Imaging Center, in an article from Nature.com, "there is not just one center in the brain. Multiple areas are interacting. There's more activity and more interactions that occur during a lie than in truth telling."

Sometimes emotions take on a life of their own and reading faces becomes even more critical, since the individual with the intense emotions may not be aware of the more subtle emotions being revealed. A very angry, or anxious, individual may miss all the subtleties of the other group members. Jaak Panksepp, in his book *Affective Neuroscience,* identified seven "semi-independent emotional command circuits" that, when activated, dominate the individual's behavior in a somewhat preprogrammed, automatic fashion. He refers to these emotions as Lust, Sorrow, Play, Rage, Seeking, Caring, and Fear.

Panksepp found that these neural "packages" seem to operate independently of the thinking brain. It's almost as if, once you switch on to a particular intense emotion—think chronic anxiety as Fear, ongoing depression as Sorrow, or losing yourself in the computer as Seeking—you have little control over the emotion itself unless you make a concerted effort to regain control. Being able to read such emotions in those around you gives you an incredible insight into how to communicate with them in a more meaningful way.

According to Roger Scruton, writing in the *Times Literary Supplement,* "Human beings are alone among the animals in revealing their individuality in their faces. The mouth that speaks, the eyes that gaze, the skin that blushes—all are signs of freedom, character and judgment, and all give concrete expression to the uniqueness of the self within." All these indications of emotion stem from the same neighborhood of the brain.

A close look at the research reveals that reading faces is a highly complex process that has a lot to do with relationships and involves at least three different areas of the brain. The only broad generalization that holds is that reading faces accurately helps improve social outcomes, and that those who are better at it also appear to exhibit stronger mirror reactions to facial expressions. In a business setting, these outcomes can mean the difference between success and failure in making the sale, managing your reports, or getting the job done under deadline as a team. That's what makes reading emotions in the faces of others in the workplace so valuable.

For better communication, learn to read face and body language. How can you enhance your sensitivity to others in the workplace? One aspect of ConnectAbility is the emotional sensitivity to be able to read facial expression, eye contact, and body expression.

Are Women Better at Reading Their Bosses' Emotions?

According to researchers Mahzarin Banaji of Harvard University and Liz Phelps of New York University, when Caucasian individuals see an African-American stranger, the amygdala reacts in a primitive response of fear. The same occurs when the races are reversed. "One of the amygdala's critical functions is fear-conditioning," says Phelps in a *Time* magazine article. "You attend to things that are scary because that's essential for survival." However, when some familiarity has time to develop, the brain cancels out the response to fear. "The more you think about people as individuals," continues Phelps, "the more the brain calms down." ConnectAbility takes into consideration the sensitivity individuals have for one another—and the related neuroscience—as they attempt to communicate at the most effective levels.

A strong argument for diversity training is made by the finding that there is an "in-group advantage" to face reading—those from the same culture read one another's faces better. African-Americans read one another's faces better than they read Caucasian faces, and vice versa. "We're 1.5 times more likely to misidentify someone from another race and 1.4 times more likely to correctly identify someone from our own," according to Christian Meissner, criminal justice professor at the University of Texas at El Paso, in a *Psychology Today* article. In addition, according to Kerry Kawakami of York University in Canada, there are more implicit biases and even more racial prejudice that exist at an unconscious level than we realize. Research has shown that cross-cultural exposure can help reduce the amount of prejudice and level "in-group advantage."[1]

The gender question again pops up: who's better at reading faces, men or women? One school of thought, known as the subordinate hypothesis, claims that women are better because they need to overcome their subordinate position by reading men more clearly. The only problem with this hypothesis is that it doesn't apply to other subordinated groups, where the opposite occurs. Other subordinated groups seem to be poorer at reading faces.

An alternative, the accommodation hypothesis, claims that there is one aspect of emotions that men are better at reading than women—feelings of

Tips for Advancing Your ConnectAbility

- **Some emotions, like ongoing depression or chronic anxiety, seem to have a life of their own and require special considerations,** especially when they interfere with normal productivity.
- **Accurately reading faces and the emotions they express is a big part of the Awareness Factor.** Those who can do so will excel at sales, management, and productive teamwork.

anger leaked through body language. For example, John might not read his wife's face too well, except when she's trying to hide her anger, which he picks up relatively easily. This dynamic increases with age.

Overlooking Your Boss's Anger

The research becomes complex when it comes to determining when women are better at reading faces. It's clear women can do it better when they're motivated. Women seem to gaze at others more than men do, enabling them to read faces better. But they seem to do so only when motivated. When married men and women are both instructed to pay explicit attention to facial behavior, the difference between the sexes begins to vanish. Ultimately, motivation plays a key role in this skill, almost overriding the differences in males and females.

According to the research of psychologists R. Rosenthal and B. M. DePaulo, reported in the *Journal of Personality and Social Psychology*, as men get older, they get better at reading anger in facial expression, while women avoid "eavesdropping" on this unintended emotional leakage. Interestingly, according to the psychologists, women who do pick up on such information seem to be less socially successful. So the wise woman who overlooks her boss's hidden anger is more likely to succeed in that relationship.

The one common factor that affects the motivation and ability to read faces is context. Although this is a proven fact, the process of context awareness is nonetheless largely unconscious. The part of the brain known as the amygdala has become well known as the site for emotional decision making, particularly when it comes to such emotions as anger and fear. It is at this site that emotional recognition of facial anger is focused and, even before the face is identified, the amygdala registers an emotional reaction if the observed face is fearful in any way. The more unconscious the perception, the more effect it has on our behavior. According to Dr. Phil Merkle of the University of Ottawa in Canada, it appears that unconsciously perceived information leads to behaviors we would otherwise be able to control if we were more aware of what we were seeing. Unconscious perception means less control over the consequent behavior.

It is the managing Performance Factor aspect of ConnectAbility that deals with knowing when to read and when to heed, in order to bring about successful outcomes. "Women have a tendency to hang back a bit in a group and think they shouldn't speak unless they have something that is either 100 percent correct or astonishingly brilliant," says Julie Hembrock Daum of Spencer Stuart in an October 2008 issue of *Newsweek*. "In a meeting or gathering, you should try to be one of the first handful of people to speak even if it is only to ask a question. If you don't, it will become harder and harder to enter the conversation." This challenge calls for a combination of both Awareness of Influence and presentation skills. Facing authentic emotions in yourself and others in the moment and sharing your awareness takes a special sensitivity to when that moment is right and when it isn't, involving select components of ConnectAbility.

Awareness of Context is usually the most important component of ConnectAbility when it comes to making decisions—whether personal or business. In the next section, you may be surprised to learn the extent to which the decisions you make rely more on your emotional reactions than your powers of intellect. As powerful as the analytical function of our brains is, our emotions can handle a lot more data and come up with a go or no-go overall feeling that is typically more accurate in the long run.

Tips for Advancing Your ConnectAbility

- **Diversity training helps overcome the "in-group advantage"** in which those within a group read others in their group better than those outside it.
- **Women are better at reading faces than men**, with the exception of reading hidden anger, at which men excel. And women who do read hidden anger are less socially successful.
- **When we're motivated to enhance our Awareness Factor and to promote our Performance Factor,** we bring otherwise unconscious processes into awareness. Intention and awareness make for greater success overall.

How Our Parents Taught Us (or Destroyed) Our ConnectAbility

The ability to acquire ConnectAbility has a lot to do with your early childhood. To the extent that you can read the faces of those in authority and apply the Awareness Factor to know how your authentic self will play out in that particular moment, you will succeed both at being seen as a positive influence and as a trustworthy, engaged associate.

As for individual differences in acquiring ConnectAbility, it appears childhood family experience has a lot to do with it. If we come from nonexpressive families, we tend to do better at reading faces, perhaps because of the need to decipher the subtleties of our parents' expressions. But if we come from violent families, then we are less adept at reading positive facial signals, perhaps because they were so rare in our early experience. Children who seem glued to the television set are also better readers of faces, though they tend to simplify the emotions they read, just as the cartoon characters they see have oversimplified and exaggerated emotions. In the end we're sensitive to the subtleties that were important to us as children.

In a *Newsweek* cover article entitled "Reading Your Baby's Mind," empathy is described as "the ability to discern emotions from the facial expressions of the people around them." Apparently, infants have that ability. According to research by LaSalle University psychology professor Diane Montague, infants can distinguish among happy, sad, and angry faces. "They seemed primed to be alert, even vigilant," according to Dr. Montague. "I think it shows that babies younger than six months find meaning in expressions." Reading others' faces is something we learn as infants. Some parents encourage it; others destroy that ability. If we were unfortunate enough to lose our innate capacity for empathy in our childhood, we can regain this "talent" if we choose to face the authentic emotions in those around us at work.

A Sense of Well-Being at Work

The emotion of happiness is such a personal concept and one that is prone to unique interpretations. Whenever I ask individuals what they want out of life, the answer is typically happiness. It is such a global term, meaning everything and nothing at the same time. I then ask what specifically would make them happy. The answers run the gamut, but one theme that stands out is the experience of connection to family, friends, and colleagues at work. Connect-Ability, of course, is the path to such feelings of connection.

Our focus here is whether or not understanding others (the Awareness Factor) and facing those aspects of yourself that are most appropriate to share (the Performance Factor) make for increased happiness or sense of well-being at work. Sharing your best public self means being in touch with your feelings. You can't be your best self if you're not in touch with your feelings. What is there to express authentically if not your inner feelings? Certainly, actions based on personal principles mean being true to yourself, but being your real, authentic self involves feelings as much as actions.

Just as the ability to read faces gives us information about others' feelings, we must read our own embodied sensations as we echo others' feelings.

It takes more than numbers to make the right decision. Even though people analyze the data—cost, benefits, and so forth—before making a business decision, the emotions are really the deciding factor.

Perhaps it's easier to read others' faces than to become cognizant of our own subtler, deeper feelings. But some of us are better at it than others.

Whether we're dealing with direct reports, colleagues, or superiors, what we communicate to them (Performance Factor) determines how effectively we influence them. The more in touch with our feelings (Awareness Factor), the research reports, the more authentically we're seen and the more receptive others are to our suggestions. So whether we're leading or following, emotional awareness is a plus. Beyond leading to effective communication, it also helps us feel better about ourselves and our interactions with others. The end result is a sense of well-being at work as well as more effective partnerships.

Business Decisions from the Gut

We know that we make decisions with emotional input, whether we're conscious of it or not. When buying a car, we analyze the costs, gas mileage, resale prospects, but at the end of the day it's the feeling we have about that car that determines what we buy. The same is true of home buying. We can analyze the cost, mortgage rates, distance to work, and so on, but again, in the end it's how we feel that determines the outcome.

Every time we meet someone new or come across a new, meaningful situation, our emotions have a lot to say about how we value that person or situation. We may think we're using our intellect, but it's the emotional brain—often at an unconscious level—that's making these decisions for us. And often it's the unconscious aspects of communication that rule. For example, it's been found that when men feel more physically dominant, "they assert themselves and their voices drop in pitch," according to Katie Gilbert, writing in *Psychology Today*. "However, when intimidated, their voices go up."

Decisions to hire and fire can be quite challenging. There are so many factors to take into consideration—personal, business, legal. To the extent that we can tap into the emotional level as to how we value the individual overall, we can enjoy the opportunity to make use of the "wisdom of the gut." Our feelings can consolidate much more data than our conscious brain. It may appear at first glance that our conscious brain has the edge, and perhaps it does in some respects, but the emotional part of the brain (and body) can do better than analysis; it can take into consideration many levels of data input and blend them all into one overarching sense of a good or bad feeling about the situation. Such a process is too overwhelming for the thinking brain alone.

When we can consciously make use of our inner feelings to make a decision, then we can make the decision much more quickly, not to mention more accurately. Otherwise, we may have to sleep on it—let our feelings emerge once our thinking process shuts down—and either dream about it or sense feelings, untainted by logic, first thing upon waking. To the extent that such feelings are unavailable to us, we make poorer decisions and judgments.

Tips for Advancing Your ConnectAbility

- **The Awareness Factor** begins in infancy. So be patient with yourself as you learn the art of ConnectAbility. It's taken a long time for your communication style to develop. If you want to change it, give yourself plenty of time.
- **Feelings determine purchase decisions** as much as logical analysis does. "Sleeping on it" makes sense if you're to give the complex emotions a chance to catch up with the linear logic of decision making.
- **Your gut** can process much more information than your "intelligent" brain. Learn to listen to your gut and, again, give it a bit of time.

> **Use your "comfort zone" for better decision making.** If there's a difficult decision to be made, after analyzing all the data, allow yourself to "sleep on it" and check your feelings about it first thing in the morning, before your logical mind can interrupt with the "facts."

We can use the term *value* to mean what we feel, positively or negatively, toward a person or situation. When we have good feelings about someone, we say we value him or her, whereas the opposite is true with bad feelings. So feelings embody value judgments. When we think we *should* like someone but don't feel the good feelings that we expect, then we experience some degree of conflict.

One of my clients recently shared why those without emotional awareness make such simplistic, rapid judgments in black and white. He revealed that anything that appeared too complex—so that it didn't fit into his clear-cut categories—made him feel very uncomfortable. Consequently, he cut things down to size so he could judge them on a more simplistic basis. It makes it easier to see how difficult business decisions are too often made on simplistic bases, sometimes sacrificing ethics and even legal considerations, leading to insurmountable problems down the road. Using the Awareness Factor in business can avoid such poor decision making. One aspect of being successful at work has to do with feeling less confusion and more clarity about life issues. Happiness is associated with finding meaning at work, while unhappiness is associated with doubt and confusion.

In a very interesting analysis, Carol Gohm and Gerald Clore divided people into four categories—hot, cool, cerebral, and overwhelmed. Hot people feel their emotions intensely, are aware of their feelings, and can talk about them accurately. Cool people are the opposite—they feel little, are unaware of any strong feelings, and have little to say about them. Cerebral types don't show their feelings but do a good job of talking about emotions. They're aware of their emotions and can discuss them but are reserved about expressing them openly and spontaneously. The overwhelmed individuals feel their emotions intensely but can't talk about them in any accurate fashion; in other words, they're confused about labeling their emotions, hence the label *overwhelmed.*

Of all four groups, the overwhelmed group appears the most complex and interesting. These individuals cannot face the reality of their feelings—they try to avoid being influenced by their emotions and end up making decisions most different from the other three groups, yet paradoxically, they report being most influenced by their moods. They mistrust their feelings, guard themselves against them, and end up with complicated decision making (or complicated outcomes). The more clearly we can describe our feelings, the happier and more effective we will become at work. The worst-case scenario is to be affected by our feelings but unable to identify them, especially when viewed through a gloomy lens.

Recent research reveals the neuroscience of happiness, validating the findings of Gohm and Clore. According to an article in *Molecular Psychiatry*, psychiatrist Martin Lepage of McGill University in Montreal found that the inability to enjoy pleasure is linked to the size of a subcortical brain region—the anterior caudate area. The smaller this area, the more likely that the "pleasure processing seems to be diverted to the logic-driven prefrontal brain region instead." As a result, these people "process these stimuli more cognitively—instead of genuinely feeling the pleasure, they have to think a little bit more about it." This sounds very much like the cool and, to some extent, the cerebral types described by Gohm and Clore.

Does ConnectAbility Lead to Fulfillment?

Facing your feelings and those of others and being your authentic self in the moment appropriately can bring success and fulfillment to work. What does the research tell us?

First of all, what does it mean to face your emotional self, to be your real self in the moment? Being your true self entails the expression of the skills inherent in ConnectAbility—empathic accuracy prior to presentation being the most important, followed by managing emotional expression. Connect-Ability includes knowing that you do indeed have the skills of self-awareness prior to presentation and that you feel comfortable using those skills. Being your authentic self means allowing the awareness of your emotions to be shared with the world *as you deem appropriate.* That's where self-presentation and empathy come into play. So, before asking if this leads to success and fulfillment, let's see if it leads to better coping skills.

Gohm and Clore tested self-reported emotional awareness against a scale of coping and found that those experiencing higher awareness were better at seeking social and emotional support and had better coping skills. Facing what's going on in yourself and in others serves you well in getting the requisite support to succeed.

Now for the critical question in this chapter: Does facing your authentic self in the moment and sharing it appropriately—the Performance Factor—and being aware of that skill and the intention to use it with the comfort of applying it—the Awareness Factor—really bring you meaning and fulfillment?

Because the answer to this question is so critical, let's have the scientists speak for themselves. Studies have shown that self-perceived emotional awareness is associated with level of happiness, percent of time spent being happy, more frequent positive affect, life satisfaction, and self-esteem. It was inversely related to general anxiety and social anxiety. In other words, facing yourself and others and the self-perceived awareness of such skills—the Awareness Factor—was highly associated with higher self-esteem, general life satisfaction, and greater happiness experienced more frequently and over longer periods of time. It was negatively associated with anxiety. Therefore, the greater the Awareness Factor, the less anxious the individual.

Note also that the authors of the study, Gohm and Clore, speculate that those who are happy find it easier to be familiar with their emotions; or that they make better decisions and better social judgments allowing them to be more comfortable being aware of their positive emotions; or that a third variable, such as self-confidence or self-esteem, may account for both the happiness and the awareness of positive emotions. In true scientific manner, all possibilities are up for consideration. But the bottom line is that those who experience a higher degree of the Awareness Factor also experience more happiness. Facing the emotions in yourself (in the context of self-presentation) and in others (empathy) is associated with more happiness, whatever the underlying mechanism.

In this chapter we've taken an in-depth look at what research has to say about the nature of how emotions are communicated in the workplace, particularly at the subtle levels that often evade our conscious awareness. Crying and laughter are particularly communicative, with laughter having special features that enhance our ability to communicate with a positive outcome. At the end of the day, the skills and management of facing what's really going on in yourself and in others, as well as in your business—the Awareness Factor—will go a long way in making you a happier person at work. The research on the matter, though complex, is consistent in proving this to be the case.

Tips for Advancing Your ConnectAbility

- **The first step in the Awareness Factor is a good or bad feeling** when first encountering a new situation. There may be shades of gray, but those are the primary feelings.
- **The more clearly you can describe your feelings**, the happier and more effective you will become. In other words, the Awareness Factor enhances success.
- **The more you consciously use your Awareness Factor skills**, the less anxious you will feel, the more support you will muster, and the higher your self-esteem will be.

CHAPTER 6

The Art of ConnectAbility

KEY 6: OVERCOME FAILURE THROUGH ACCEPTANCE

Accept when a situation or interaction has gone wrong and reframe it to discover the "silver lining." Instead of becoming overwhelmed by anxiety, permit yourself to experience the emotion in the moment by focusing on it and labeling it accurately, allowing yourself to return to a state of inner calm (or mindfulness). Only then will you regain your self-confidence, integrity, and ability to be more persuasive and generally effective with others—colleagues or customers—at work.

THE AWARENESS FACTOR has a lot to do with accepting the truth of what is in the moment. Being your fully aware self in the workplace is not emotional transparency. It is a maturely developed sense of your deeper values expressed in your communication with others. It is an awareness of others and a respect for their perspectives integrated into the expression of your inner values. Beyond that, it can also include a sense of optimism to make your communication even more effective for yourself and your organization.

Reframing is one way of infusing optimism into your everyday thinking. Reframing means rearranging your point of view so that it transforms, generally, from a negative to a positive outcome. It often means creating a positive spin to increase your options for a desirable outcome. Three such spins have been identified by psychologists: (1) positive reappraisal (finding a "silver lining"), (2) problem-focused coping, and (3) infusing ordinary events with positive meaning (e.g., appreciating the beauty of the moment). Research has shown that these Awareness Factor perspectives result in less stress and more positive emotion. They also result in fewer physical symptoms of stress.

All this falls in line with what psychologists refer to as the "broaden-and-build" theory, which maintains that if you can keep your head when all about you are losing theirs, to paraphrase Rudyard Kipling, then you will have more options available in your mental problem-solving resources. In other words, if you allow yourself to fall into a fight-or-flight mode, you become more defensive, worried, and narrow in your thinking. On the other hand, if you can reframe the challenge so that you become more detached from the anxiety and see the situation in a more objective light, with an optimistic outlook, then your body relaxes, your brain operates more effectively, and there are more options from which to choose. Think of the bosses you've worked for over your career. When challenges came calling and there was reason to batten down the hatches, how did your boss react? The best bosses do not lose their heads but rather take the long-range view and put things in their proper perspective.

Learn the art of reframing bad situations. Three ways of reframing bad outcomes are (1) finding the "silver lining," (2) focusing on solving the problem, and (3) appreciating the moment, with what it has to teach us, even when bad things happen. Then move ahead creatively, garnering support from your helpful associates.

Regulating Emotions for Creative Problem Solving

What this is all about is subsumed under one of the components of the Performance Factor, agility skills—in this case, emotional control or regulation of emotions in consideration of others' reactions. To the extent that you can control or regulate the negative emotions that arise throughout your workday, you can function more effectively and maintain better health by decreasing your level of stress.

It's clear that some people are better at this emotional regulation skill than others. So how do you assure that you're one of those who are skilled at it? The answer lies in an important aspect of agility skills—your experience of mindfulness, the ability to bring objective awareness to your inner self as you cope. This objective awareness gives you enough distance from the primal anxiety that might otherwise prevail so that you can relax sufficiently to bring your intellectual resources to bear. Only through a continuing practice of mindfulness can you trust yourself to be calm at any moment, even those moments fraught with great challenge. Research shows that those who have this ability, inherent in the Performance Factor, to maintain their cool in the face of great challenge and have the resilience to stay positive when others are stressed out are able to restore their self-esteem much more quickly, demonstrate more creative problem solving, and make good use of social support networks to help them deal with the challenges at hand.

Being in the moment is one component of this form of resiliency. By being mindful in the moment, we experience more openness to the various shades of emotion that pass through our awareness. Yes, certain challenges do cause anxiety, but there are also shades of excitement and wonder that pass through moments of awareness, even in the dire circumstances that might prevail. Capturing and focusing on such passing, positive emotions offers the flexibility and resilience to change negative feelings into positive ones.

Right now you're probably thinking, "Sure, all this sounds great. But how many of us really have the ability to keep a cool head when stress is the order of the day? Some people are just luckier than others or are born that way and maybe I'm not one of them. When I'm stressed, I'm stressed; and capturing the positive thoughts as they pass through my mind isn't very likely to happen." You're quite right in that it isn't easy for most people. As it turns out, some people are more adept at this than others—some just seem to be born "lucky." But there is a way to become one of the "lucky" ones, and that is to make a choice to practice the art of mindful awareness. Whatever framework of self-discipline you choose, it involves the choice to become more objectively aware of your experience as you interact with others.

As a matter of fact, recent research on the brain reveals that it is possible to control how our brain performs just by making the decision to take control. We can control, to some extent, not only the electrical circuitry of our brains but its biochemical functioning as well. According to neuroscientist Elisabeth Perreau-Linck of the University of Montreal, who measured the serotonin synthesis capacity (SSC) of her human subjects via a PET scan, those who self-induced states of sadness had brain scans markedly different from those who didn't. "We found that healthy individuals are capable of consciously and voluntarily modulating SSC by transiently altering their emotional state," she reported in a presentation before the Society for Neuroscience. "In essence, people have the capacity to affect the electrochemical dynamics of their brains by changing the nature of their mind process."

A Brief History of Emotions

More than 150 years ago, Charles Darwin satisfied his curiosity about emotions by examining how they were expressed in animals. Being human, he was somewhat limited in his ability to distinguish the intricacies and subtleties of animal emotional expression. He settled for two: smiling approval and frowning disapproval. If you think of your own pets' emotional expression, that's not bad for starters. If not for wagging tails, dogs would be even more discrete about their happiness. But a fierce growl with bared teeth leaves little doubt about feelings. Cats are a bit more demure about their inner selves. But, even absent purring or quick swipes of their claws, we can still sense whether they're happy or not by their facial expression.

More recently, scientists specializing in emotions have expanded the number of basic emotions to six: happiness, sadness, anger, fear, disgust, and surprise. Jaak Panksepp, as mentioned in Chapter 5, found seven "emotional packages": Seeking, Caring, Play, and Lust on the positive side, and Rage, Fear, and Sorrow on the negative side. According to Panksepp, any of these "packages" can persevere until they're "turned off" by a decisive action. In other words, we can get lost in Rage or Lust, as these emotions are known to overwhelm more thoughtful considerations. But we can also get lost in Seeking, as when time "disappears" as we focus on the Internet or a great book or research. We often see professional athletes or Olympians play through a broken bone, seemingly unaware of the pain, as they get lost in the "emotional package" of Play. Sorrow can go on and on without abatement when depression stakes its claim in our ongoing lives.

So, to the extent that Panksepp's theory of emotions holds water, it is clearly not easy to regulate some of our emotions, particularly when they take hold and we don't manage them. On the other hand, if we can make use of our Awareness of Self, perhaps using the skills of mindfulness, and then use our agility skills to focus on an emotion of our choice before our feelings become too intense and absorbing, then we have greater control over them. A basic understanding of the neurology of the brain helps us to make even more sense of this.

Tips for Advancing Your ConnectAbility

- **Make the best of any challenging situation by reframing it**, or focusing on the solution to the problem rather than on the hardship.
- **Mindfulness, or the ability to stay calm in the light of extreme challenge**, is one aspect of agility skills. To use it you must focus intently on the present moment, particularly on the emotions you feel, but from a calm, detached perspective.
- **We can control our emotions**, but only if we learn to be highly aware of them and choose to adapt to changing circumstances quickly and decisively.

Maintaining Your Cool in Times of Stress

Suffice it to say that a small organ in the side of your brain—the amygdala, which we've talked about in previous chapters—is the center of emotional decision making. To simplify, the neurons sending messages from the amygdala to the thinking brain, or the prefrontal cortex, are easy to travel. On the other hand, the neurons going from the thinking brain to the amygdala, in the opposite direction, are not easy traveling. Think of it as a superhighway from the amygdala to the thinking part of the brain and a rough, dirt road, overwhelmed with growth, from the thinking brain to the amygdala. That means that it's relatively easy to sense what we're feeling (via the "superhighway"), but dreadfully difficult to change what we're feeling with mere thought alone (via the overgrown dirt road)—not impossible, just very, very challenging.

On the other hand, sometimes mere thoughts can trigger certain emotions. Do you want to have a nice, warm feeling? Then think of spending undisturbed, relaxed time with someone who loves you dearly. Do you want to feel a sudden surge of anxiety-producing adrenaline? Then picture a nasty rat running helter-skelter across the room and scampering in panic up your leg. Or imagine receiving a certified letter from the IRS. Or a call from your significant other, beginning with a brief pause, and then, in hushed tone, "We have to talk."

What's so interesting is that even though it's relatively easy to get the adrenaline rush, it's not so easy to get rid of it. That's because it involves a cycle of events that tends to persevere at least for a while. The rat or certified letter or hushed tone and message trigger the amygdala to fight-or-flight mode. This triggers the pituitary gland, at the base of your brain, to release stress hormones that, when they reach the kidneys a heartbeat or three later, trigger the glands seated above the kidneys to release noradrenaline, which gets the heart beating faster and initiates a whole host of physical defense mechanisms. Even if the initial stimulus was an error of perception (merely a few words in a book rather than the real thing, or a scene in a horror flick), the fear persists for a while.

At the risk of oversimplifying, it can be stated that the brain is divided into a more rational, thinking mode—the left brain—and the more emotional, intuitive, creative side—the right brain. Paradoxically, when fear is activated, it's in the left brain. Perhaps it's the fear arousing in us the need to prepare for the worst that engages the thinking aspect of the brain. What to do in case of emergency is just as important as the recognition of the threat itself. This thinking aspect also gives us the opportunity to rethink or reappraise a situation so that if the threat is more imagined than real, we can reinterpret the challenge we're facing and react appropriately. Think of the emotion aroused by a terrifying movie scene and then reminding yourself that it's only a movie. Reappraisal can actually change the brain activity so that we become less stressed. Sometimes just putting a name to a threatening situation, that is, labeling it, can reduce the stress reaction in our brain.

As the amygdala (recognizing and reacting to threat with "fear" hormones) struggles with the rational frontal cortex as to which will dominate—fear or relatively calm thoughtfulness—reappraising the situation leads the battle to a more victorious frontal cortex. According to UCLA neuroscientist Golnaz Tabibnia, labeling a threatening situation activates the prefrontal cortex and reduces the emotional circuitry of the brain. Tabibnia and colleagues showed photos of angry faces and recorded the brain reactions of the subjects. Then the subjects were instructed to label the faces as "angry." This had the effect of decreasing the amygdala reaction and fortifying the return to a calmer thinking process of the prefrontal cortex. Somehow, just the linguistic mechanism of labeling something in its category soothes the "frightened" brain and provides a sense of control over the situation.[1]

It has also been shown by Canadian neuroscanner Mario Beauregard, working at the University of Montreal, that voluntarily suppressing sad feelings will change the fMRIs of individuals. Dr. Beauregard asked women to view a series of sad film excerpts and recorded their fMRIs. What came up was the expected firing up of areas of the brain known to be triggered by sadness. However, when he instructed his subjects to voluntarily suppress their feelings of sadness, their hypothalamus (a part of the brain heavily involved in emotion) became less engaged, proving the powerful effects that thinking can sometimes have over emotions of sadness. It's interesting to note, though, that younger females (age 8 to 10) did not have this same ability. Apparently, reasoned Dr. Beauregard, the prefrontal cortex is not fully developed at that age, and it appears that only the fully developed prefrontal cortex (in adulthood) has this capacity to attenuate sadness through "thought control."[2]

Still stressed? Just stick a label on it! Research at UCLA has shown that just being able to apply a label to some very stressful emotion reduces the stress level and allows us to respond more positively.

So emotions, to the extent that they have a life of their own, are not easy to manage. It's a lot easier to regulate good feelings, but much more challenging to regulate fear and anxiety. That's why so many of us are so quick to rely on pharmaceuticals to regulate unpleasant emotions. And here's where mindfulness pays off. By creating a buffer zone between signals from the real world and our own vulnerable brain, we can reduce a substantial amount of felt threat.

Mindfulness creates a protective barrier between our sensibilities and the rough-and-tumble world "out there." We can counter the threat signals by saying something like, "Oh, how interesting that my heart is beating fast and my body feels tensed up just because that rat is scampering up my leg. / I just got a certified letter from the IRS. / My dear one has something dreadful to tell me! I'm aware of feeling the fear that's building up. Let's see what the next moment will bring, so I can feel my awareness of that as well."

It may sound silly, but it works. Feeling in the moment allows you to track your feelings rather than get paralyzed in the first moment of fear. It gives you that extra distance—even if it's only a little bit—to be open to the next moment and the next, which will probably dissipate some of that fear, so long as you don't get locked into the "neural package" of Fear that Panksepp describes. Mindfulness keeps the "neural packages" from taking over and persevering.

Creating Your Own "Luck"

With the discipline of the Awareness Factor, it's much easier to bring into play the three reframing "spins" mentioned earlier in the chapter. When you

Use the awareness factor to gain fulfillment. The formula for finding fulfillment at work is as follows: Fulfillment = sense of feeling (appreciated/unique/respected) + sense of serving others + giving back (to community or organization). All these components of the equation are enhanced by the Awareness Factor.

are not paralyzed by fear of anxiety, but rather focusing on it in a mindful, detached manner, you're much more likely to be able to reframe threatening situations. Mindful awareness is like a rest stop where you can look over your cognitive map (examine how you're thinking), reorganize your feelings, or reframe them. That's how you build your coping skills, decrease your feelings of stress, and uncover positive feelings. Those agility skills, in turn, lead to better health overall as well as help you to deal with business crises in the moment.

In line with the broaden-and-build theory mentioned earlier, once the paralyzing effect of fear is overcome, you can dig into your repertoire of positive choices to improve your situation and end up looking "lucky" to the casual observer, because you come out of the threat with a sense of control and positive feelings. To be clear, we are not recommending ignoring your feelings. Rather, it is the ability to be acutely aware of your ongoing feelings from moment to moment as well as how your thoughts influence your feelings that we are advocating. Awareness of your feelings, in addition to contributing to your comfort level, gives you added information as to what to do next. You aim for a greater comfort level in order to explore the options that you can now bring to fruition with a calmer mind, paying more attention to your intuition.

Richard Wiseman, author of *The Luck Factor*, stated in an article in *Newsweek*, "My interviews suggested that lucky people's gut feelings and hunches tended to pay off time and time again. In contrast, unlucky people often ignore their intuition and regret their decision." According to Wiseman, only 10 percent of what happens to you in life is purely random. The rest—90 percent—is "actually defined by what you think." He offers four keys to create your own "luck":

1. Relax and allow yourself to be more aware of your environment for opportunities from which you can benefit.
2. Listen carefully to your hunches, even if you don't understand where they come from.
3. Even when you seem to be facing failure, persevere. Says Wiseman: "The unlucky people gave up before they even started."
4. Make use of what you've just learned about reframing in this chapter as well as the preceding one. Get into that "silver lining" that comes with apparent misfortune. According to Dr. Al Siebert, an eminent expert on survival psychology, "Life's best survivors not only cope well, they often turn potential disaster into a lucky development." This ability to turn apparent bad luck into good fortune, according to Wiseman, plays a very important role in surviving threatening circumstances. So reframing has great advantages when you learn how to use it.

What we haven't mentioned so far is the importance of having a sense of your overall intention. To ask what your values are seems a bit abstract. Perhaps it might be easier to ask what is important to you—either in a general sense or in a particular situation. One of the easier value systems from which to operate is that of being of service to others. Integrity then becomes automatic. If your intention is to be of service to others, having taken care of your own basic needs first, of course, then decisions are much easier to make. There is inherently less conflict in your dealings with people. You automatically become closer to others, meeting that need for social support. People tend to like you more as they sense your "giving" nature.

A healthy lifestyle involves the practice of being intentional in your dealings with others, not only to serve them but also to have your own needs met in an uncomplicated, ongoing manner. So what are your needs?

Tips for Advancing Your ConnectAbility

- **Although the fight-or-flight response can take over if we let it, labeling the feeling** or the situation arousing it gives us a much better chance of overcoming that anxiety.
- **Focusing intently on the emotion in the moment and labeling it helps us become much calmer**, even if that emotion is anxiety. Try this to keep your cool in any business crisis.
- **To build a sense of integrity in business relationships**, foster the value of being of service to others.

According to Abraham Maslow, a major pioneer in bringing emotional awareness to the workplace and best known for his concept of the Hierarchy of Needs, humans must begin by fulfilling their basic needs: healthy air, food and water, protection from the elements. Social contact and the need to feel loved are next. Then we need to feel unique, important, respected, and, finally, to give back or serve. Many of us can take the basics such as food and shelter for granted. Feeling loved starts with genuine relationships at home and continues with friends, networks, and associates, the intensity decreasing the farther from home. Feeling unique and valued comes to a significant extent from being your real self in the moment. It all begins to fit together: awareness of your moment-to-moment feelings, positive coping skills that are assisted by mindful awareness, a clear sense of your purpose in life as an expression of your deeper values, and, finally, a sense of meaning coming from your unique offerings to others.

The result of such an approach to life means better outcomes no matter what the challenges because of greater personal insights. If you can manage the Awareness Factor and use the resulting insight to choose service as a broad value, then you'll be more optimistic, more zestful, more open to new experiences, and happier. It also means you'll be likely to bounce back from stressful experiences more efficiently and quickly. As mentioned earlier, you'll be more likely to grasp the positive aspects of your emotion, even when dealing with anxiety in a stress-inducing challenge.

Some psychologists make a sharp distinction between the concepts of challenge and threat. Threat is seen as something we can't overcome, while challenge is seen as something we can. If you can interpret the trials and demands of life as surmountable because of the Awareness Factor and intention to serve, then threats will be converted to challenges. If you can keep your mind full of awareness when those around you are giving in to the paralysis of fear and anxiety, then you can conquer the demons that have trapped you in the past. Anxiety is the modern-day demon that haunts our every workday, if we allow it.

But you have choices. Broaden your basis of agility skills. Feel free to reframe threats into challenges. See the possibilities for success that evaded you before. Such choices, creatively tuned, build on themselves. Your future is predicated by present declarations. Using ConnectAbility in the workplace, with all the specific skills explored in this chapter, will only brighten your future.

CHAPTER 7

Mastering Your Emotions with Confidence

KEY 7: MAINTAIN AWARENESS OF EMOTIONAL DYNAMICS

In developing strong partnerships with your colleagues and customers, master the emotional dynamics of every conversation you have. There are six basic categories of emotions: happiness and surprise (labeled "good"), and anger, disgust, sadness, and fear (labeled "bad"). Bad emotions can best be dealt with by acknowledging them to yourself and labeling them accurately. You can then feel free to share this newfound awareness, if appropriate—this will predictably decrease the intensity. Authentic awareness in the service of supporting others will only help bring about the best outcome in any form of communication.

PAUL IS THE chief financial officer of a fast-growing manufacturing company. He is liked by everyone at work, especially his boss, and he is flawless in getting his job done to everyone's satisfaction. He has a wonderful family—a conscientious wife, two school-age children, and a chocolate

Labrador that keeps the family smiling. Paul and his wife, Sharon, are the perfect couple to the outside world, unless they're having one of their occasional spats. They love staying up late and talking till two in the morning on weekends or holidays, sharing Sunday brunch at the local funky restaurant, and walking their dog in the nearby park. But their spats sometimes turn intense.

One day, during a family gathering, while Sharon was reading a book, Paul began playing cards with her sister, who was visiting. Sharon finished her reading, but Paul was still involved in the card game. Sensitive to feeling rejected, Sharon blew up. The fight led to reconciliation, but these fights were becoming more and more frequent and exacerbated.

After one fight, Paul's patience was finally taken to the limit. Frustrated, he smashed his fist through the wall, and as he made an angry retreat from their home, he slammed the door shut behind him, breaking its lead-paned glass panel. The end result of this "spat" was his moving out and the sheriff handing him a temporary restraining order to stay away from Sharon.

Clearly, there were some bad feelings here. And Paul could not keep these bad feelings from affecting his relationships at work. He was surly with his associates, barked at his office staff. This was not the Paul everyone knew. Unless Paul could patch up his home situation, he was on the verge of losing all the respect of his associates that had built up over the years.

Sometimes it's hard to separate home life from work. If we leave home in the morning all tied up with stress, that's how we'll arrive—and possibly remain—at work. Paul had to do something. But bad feelings are bad feelings. It's what we do with them, using our ConnectAbility skills, that makes the difference. So how could Paul and Sharon have made better use of these bad feelings?

Good and Bad Emotions

In the previous chapter, we looked at how it's possible to reframe perceptions so that the positive is allowed to emerge from challenging situations. Con-

Start with the basics—the difference between good and bad.
Sometimes emotions can overwhelm us with their social complexity. One way of narrowing this down is to realize that emotions come in two basic flavors—good and bad feelings. The rest is determined by context, expectations, priorities, and a host of other factors. But it helps to start with the basics—knowing what's good and what's bad.

nectAbility offers a framework in which we can use our minds to regulate our feelings. It is that combination of mind and emotion that allows us to be our best socially intelligent self in the moment.

Emotions come in two basic flavors—good and bad. All our feelings are variations on that basic theme. But we can manage bad emotions so that even they can help us be more effective. Not by reframing them, but by using them in their basic form to guide us to better choices.

For starters, negative emotions offer us signals as to what to avoid. They may not tell us how to do so, when to do so, or what measures to take, but they do tell us something is wrong with this picture.

Emotions as Traffic Signals

Could Paul and Sharon have made better use of their negative emotions? To begin to answer that question, let's look at some basics. Emotions, good or bad, have at least the function of giving meaning to the events leading up to the emotion—whether our reaction is good or bad. One way of putting it is that every emotion, metaphorically speaking, comes with its own traffic light—red, yellow, or green. The more intense the emotion, the more vivid and intense the colors. Red obviously tells us something is wrong. It tells us we're under threat or our actions are leading to failure or others are judging us poorly. Green tells us the opposite—we're succeeding or people are supporting us. Yellow tells us we don't have enough information, but things aren't looking so good and we should use caution.

Emotions convey the value of the experiences they accompany. They can be used as clear markers on the path of life. As we drive along a road, we may see a sign saying, "Bridge Ahead." We can see the bridge ahead as we approach it, even if we're not looking carefully, but we may be distracted, so the sign gives us a bit of warning. Similarly, a sign warning us of a traffic signal ahead seems wasted—we certainly can't miss the traffic signal when we get there—but that sign gives us a bit more time to prepare to slow down.

The social parallel exists. Emotions, particularly the bad ones, prepare us for what seems obvious once we get a bit farther down the road. How might Paul and Sharon have made better use of their negative emotions? One answer is obvious: they might have gone to some form of counseling before the poor communication between them led to a sheriff's arrival with legal papers. The emotions didn't tell them to do exactly that; they simply alerted them that something was wrong.

More than mere signals of good and bad, emotions can have some specificity in terms of how to react. Anxiety says: "Watch out! You may have to get away quickly." Anger says: "Get ready to attack! You need to defend yourself." Embarrassment says: "Uh-oh! You sure messed up here. Maybe you better lay low for a while." Sadness says: "You're not doing so well here. Maybe you ought to give up or take a break."

Learn how to read your emotional signals. Emotions can be used like traffic lights. Green (happiness) says things are OK and that we're in sync with others; move ahead at full speed. Yellow (embarrassment, sadness) tells us we don't have enough information, and that things aren't looking too good; slow down! Red (anger, anxiety) says something is clearly wrong. Our judgment is off and failure looks probable. Stop now and consider your next move.

Don't just react; instead, reflect. Instead of striking out at someone, what are the most productive questions you can bring to the table? Instead of withdrawing, to whom can you go to get support? Instead of giving up, how can you reframe the situation to achieve your goals? In general, bad emotions can be useful if we handle them with mindfulness.

Impulsive Disregard or Mindful Awareness

How would Paul and Sharon manifest such emotions? When Sharon felt angry with Paul for continuing to play cards and ignoring her, her emotional reaction might have made her appear "snappish." Paul, fearing another fight, might appear jumpy. After a fight, the resulting sadness might make both appear subdued and withdrawn. So even though emotions don't give us specifics on how to react, they certainly do give us signs of what might be appropriate, in a general sense, to the situation at hand.

Paul and Sharon could have used their emotions in another way as well. When Sharon was peeved at Paul's "ignoring" her, she felt "snappish" and her first reaction was to fight with him. If she had been mindful of her emotions rather than acting on them, she might have acknowledged, first to herself and then to Paul, that she was feeling angry at being ignored. Her saying this in a calm manner might have defused the whole situation if Paul had chosen to give her some attention at that point.

When Paul was acting jumpy, he could have used that feeling to be more sensitive to Sharon's needs and avoid any fights. Since they didn't choose such actions, a fight ensued. After the fight, both withdrew emotionally and began aggressively talking about how they should be apart from one another. Had they chosen to be more mindful and share their authentic selves with one another, they might have said how hurt they felt and that they only felt so vulnerable because of their love for one another. That might have led to some deep sharing and a closer connection with revelations of one another's needs being taken into better consideration.

Notice how often we used the phrases "might have" and "could have." There's no certainty that reacting any particular way to these negative emotions would end up in happiness. But the probabilities are greater. Negative emotions give us general clues but not specific instructions.

Moving Forward with Confidence

In a work setting, the same principles apply. If Paul had applied for a promotion and then found out that he didn't get it, his negative reaction would probably be anger at his boss, sadness at the disappointment, and anxiety about his career arc. Rather than lash out at his boss or act snappish with co-workers, rather than withdraw from his assignments by losing himself in a card game on his PC, rather than giving up on his pet project, Paul might have a serious chat with his boss about his career aspirations and how he might make a better fit within the organization. He might ask for assignments that are more closely linked to his likings and aptitudes, and he might put even more energy into his pet project to feel better about making a unique offering to the organization. By being his authentic self to his boss, he might improve his career path by making a better fit.

Tips for Advancing Your ConnectAbility

- **Emotions can be broken down into two groups—good and bad.** Learn to recognize the signals as useful signs of what works for you and what doesn't.
- **Each of the six basic emotions serves to signal us of what lies ahead.** Learn the language of your own emotions.
- **To defuse intense negative emotions, label them and become aware or mindful of them.** Then, if appropriate, share your awareness. The negative intensity predictably decreases.

This seems like such an obvious choice, yet one taken so rarely by most of us. Why is that? Because these negative emotions in themselves are not indications of what we should do except in a very general, vague sense. The choices we make are based on clear thinking about our lives. The emotions are mere signposts indicating the general disposition of our reactions.

Do we lash out when we feel anger, as is our first inclination, or do we acknowledge our frustration in a more mindful manner? Do we run away when we fear something, or do we mindfully share that fear with a supportive individual who might help us come up with a more productive solution? Do we withdraw from someone we love when hurt, or do we choose to be our real self in the moment and share as openly as we can how hurt we feel because of our vulnerability to that special person? The answers to these questions require mindful thought and openness. The emotions themselves don't give us the answers. But they are priceless as signposts.

In general, bad emotions can be useful if we handle them with mindfulness—as indications for the need to pay more attention to whatever provokes such emotions and to react with more thoughtfulness than usual. Our first inclinations—striking out, withdrawing, giving up—are probably not the best. It's the balance between emotion and mind that gives us the advantage. Instead of striking out, we can move forward in a more appropriate manner with more confidence. Instead of withdrawing, we can seek out support to bolster our lagging confidence. Instead of giving up, we can reframe our aspirations to better fit the environment we find ourselves in.

Learn the four steps of awareness reflection. Reflecting on a problem with mindful awareness involves four steps: (1) acknowledging the feeling, whatever it is; (2) understanding the context in which it occurred; (3) taking responsibility for our reaction by strategizing the most productive options; and (4) moving ahead with the response that serves us and the other party best.

High-Tech Rejection or Reality Awareness

Once in a while, we may choose to go along with our first inclinations, if that appears to be the right thing after giving it due consideration. Anger might be used as fuel to move ahead on a stalled project. Letting a customer go may be the right thing if, after thoughtful consideration, it appears that the return on investment no longer makes sense.

On the other hand, sometimes our emotional reactions are due to false readings. How often do you wonder if someone has screened your call when all you get, call after call, is voice mail? How often do you feel rejected when your e-mails go unanswered? It seems high-tech communication can lead to high-tech rejection. Similarly, in a social setting, have you ever wondered why you're not approached more frequently at the reception before a business meeting? Could it be that you haven't bothered to approach anyone yourself? No, you conclude, probably falsely, it's that you're not liked.

Unfortunately, our emotions of withdrawal to such settings don't know the difference between normal paranoia and reality. What if you're talking with someone who is using a cell phone, and suddenly the line goes dead, just when you were asking a special favor? The normal emotional reaction takes little heed of the fact that it might have been an electronic glitch. Again, bad emotions can't tell the difference between reality and illusion of rejection.

False Priorities

You ask a new employee out to lunch, hoping to establish a link with someone who has an expertise that is very useful to you. However, this person turns you down without any specific explanation and without reference to a future lunch date. You might end up feeling at least some sadness, no matter how mindful you are in the habit of the Awareness Factor. So you spend the free moments of the afternoon contemplating how this individual really isn't that important to you, or why he or she might have turned you down.

Now, what if this person couldn't make that lunch date but would have if he or she didn't have another appointment? This person just assumed another lunch date would be forthcoming and didn't bother mentioning it then and there. All that postrejection fussing on your part was wasted time and may have impaired an otherwise productive relationship. The most effective response to this would be a survey of how often you feel such rejection. If, after honest appraisal, you come up with an inordinate number of times, then it's a good guess that the rejection has more to do with your overactive feelings of rejection than of others truly rejecting you. In such a case, you need to be more wary of initial feelings of rejection in the future. On the other hand, if they occur rarely, then consider that life has uncertainties that sometimes cause unwarranted negative feelings.

A very dysfunctional choice occurs when some negative emotion causes us to pay more attention to something that matters little in the long run while ignoring more important items. Some negative emotions can have an obsessive quality if we allow them to. If one project seems to be failing and we assign it a high priority just because we want to avoid failure when a more objective perspective would reveal it is of minimal importance when compared with other high-priority projects, then a reassessment is in order. We need to be wary of emotions leading us astray just because of fear of failure. Sometimes comparing notes with others can be of great help in overcoming the urgent quality of certain negative emotions. Mindful reflection and "picking others' brains" can give us the distance needed from the false priorities given because of the urgency of emotions.

The Four Steps to Awareness Resolution

So how do people like Paul and Sharon best deal with emotions? There are four stages to emotional awareness:

1. **Impulsive reaction.** Initially we experience the emotion and react blindly and impulsively—the tendency to strike out with anger, to flee from anxiety, or to give up when disappointed or sad.
2. **Creating context.** The second stage consists of putting that emotion in the social context that gave rise to it. Anger becomes aimed at someone

or something explicit, perhaps tinged with envy. Fear becomes a reaction to some threat. Sadness becomes a reaction to some disappointment, possibly mixed with jealousy. Here we build a "cognitive model" of what is happening to us, often a dramatic story line with ourselves as the main character. It's what Joseph LeDoux, author of *The Emotional Brain*, calls taking the "high road"—through the thinking cortex—instead of the "low road"—from perception directly to the emotional portion of the brain.

3. **Mindful awareness.** The next stage involves being mindful of the emotion so that the best and most productive decision can be made. In this stage we can begin to take personal responsibility for the events leading up to the negative emotion and try to put the most objective perspective into play. In addition, we begin to assess how others might react to any display of emotion (or lack thereof) on our part. Mindfulness plays a significant role in this stage as we appraise the best strategy for productive outcome, given the emotions in question. In neuroscientific terms, the "thinking" frontal cortex of the brain begins to take over from the emotion-laden amygdala. According to Mario Beauregard of the University of Montreal, "we humans have the capacity to consciously and voluntarily modulate the electrical and chemical functioning of our brains by voluntarily changing the nature of our brain process."[1]

4. **Awareness resolution.** The fourth stage is the decision to move ahead with the best and most appropriate action, one that integrates our authentic self with the sensibilities of what would work best for all involved parties.

Creating a Mindful Context

So how might Paul and Sharon have benefited from all this knowledge? Recall that fight from earlier in which Paul continued playing cards with Sharon's sister, even though Sharon had finished reading and was ready to interact with Paul. Sharon felt angry. Instead of lashing out at him, she could have put that anger in context, realized that she was responsible for ignoring Paul as she turned to her reading, and decided to allow Paul to finish his game while at the same time inviting him to interact with her as soon as he was finished. Reappraising the situation from anger to a calmer perspective of personal responsibility would have a dramatic effect on her brain function, transforming the predominance of left-sided amygdala—registering fear—to the more "thoughtful" frontal cortex—where calm and awareness prevail. Just taking the larger perspective, the more thoughtful one that allows for putting oneself in the other person's shoes, transforms upset feelings into calm ones.

One road to attaining the calmer perspective is the mere process of labeling a situation, somehow giving us a sense of control over it. According to UCLA neuroscientist Golnaz Tabibnia, simply labeling and identifying our negative emotions give us a sense of mastery over them. "The prefrontal cortex [where thinking takes place] attenuates responses in the brain's emotion centers," remarked Tabibnia at an annual meeting of the Society for Neuroscience. "That's why emotion labeling may help us reduce emotional responses in the long term." For his part, Paul, if the fight had taken place, could have felt upset by Sharon's anger, put that episode in context, and realized that Sharon needed his attention, having chosen to let him know by her display of anger. He could then have chosen to share his mindful awareness

Tips for Advancing Your ConnectAbility

- **The Awareness Factor helps to control negative emotions.** Be mindful of your emotions rather than reacting impulsively.
- **"Virtual rejection" occurs when digital glitches interrupt our electronic communications at vulnerable points.** Be mindful of how easy it is to personalize such electronic interruptions.
- **Controlling intense emotions involves a number of steps**, but the basis is the Awareness Factor.

of all this with her and proceeded to show her affection and caring as an expression of his love.

Is this account too idealistic? Perhaps. Somewhere between lashing out with anger and awareness resolution lies the reality of the situation. The more discipline you have toward ConnectAbility, the closer you get to the ideal of mindfulness leading to a calm overview. Paul, Sharon, you, and I—we all deserve to be respected and treated with genuine honesty. It may be a lot to ask for, but life is short and every moment counts. So why not act with ConnectAbility in those valuable moments? Be your authentic self with others and chances are much better that others will return the favor.

CHAPTER 8

Connecting with Optimism

KEY 8: CHALLENGE YOURSELF BY TAKING CHARGE

No matter how challenging a situation, even those that seem impossible to control, whether with your colleagues or with customers, your best approach is to be realistic about the details, take charge, and aim for the best. In addition, be realistic about your authentic feelings and use the skills you've learned to deal with them appropriately. As you engage others toward the best solution, demonstrate ongoing appreciation for their efforts. That completes the loop of using relationship dynamics for the best connecting.

ONE STORY THAT remains with me from my student days—referred to as the "Pygmalion" effect, based on research by Robert Rosenthal and Lenore Jacobson in 1965—involves one group of teachers who are told that their students are ready for a growth spurt according to test results while another group of teachers are not told that. The study involved students in grades 1 though 6 in a San Francisco elementary school. The point was to determine if teacher expectations of student success created a self-fulfilling prophecy. Could such expectations affect student achievement? The students in both groups were by and large equal in their intellect, yet—you guessed it—the first group of students subsequently performed much better than the second group. Why? Expectation, in a word. When we truly expect the best in others, we are more likely to find it, see it achieved, and experience it. That's one reason optimism works.

So, having underscored the importance of meaningfulness and optimism, how does someone like yourself accomplish these in your own life? The starting point is emotional awareness, first of your own authentic self and then of those around you. Emotions are the currency of good interpersonal connection. Meaning comes from finding value in your experience of life, primarily in the relationships with those with whom you interact on a daily basis. Optimism is the result of taking hold of the uncertainties that life offers you and creating success by taking charge of the details under your control.

What about the claim that optimists just deny the gravity of harsh reality? It turns out that, on close inspection, even in the face of disaster optimists are less crushed than pessimists. Some time ago a young, beautiful supermodel was interviewed on TV by Larry King. This woman had been a victim of the tragic tsunami of 2004—suffering physically with many broken bones—while visiting Thailand during a trip that she had given to her boyfriend as a gift. The tragedy was that she also lost her boyfriend to the tsunami. Yet her high spirits continued to soar. Sure, she grieved his passing, but then she went on to celebrate his life with other loved ones in their circle and was on her way back to Thailand to thank the medical community for helping her with her own injuries and to see what she could do for the affected community in that area. Her positive nature was astounding. She was living proof that optimism works.

How does an optimist differ from a pessimist? Most of us are familiar with the credo to change what we can, accept what we can't, and "have the wisdom to know the difference." The wisdom of the pessimist usually errs on the side of "can't," while the optimist is earnest in changing almost anything, unwilling to yield to the "can't" category. The pessimist plays up the possible negative outcomes; the optimist takes charge in creating positive outcomes. A pessimist loses energy quickly when faced with a challenge; the optimist creates a momentum that is not easily stopped. The optimist looks for what is possible to change and dives right in with energetic zeal. Once a complete attempt has been made to change a situation for the better, only then does the optimist accept what cannot be changed and does so with equanimity.

Here's what we believe about optimism: We're basically optimists. We believe that what's around the corner is going to be good, or that getting past the next hurdle will lead us to something pleasant. We live by the mantra "This too shall pass" when dealing with negative situations and savor and enjoy our blessings daily. We're grateful and, consciously, we count our blessings. We notice the good in everything and remind ourselves to continue this practice.

The pessimist hopes something bad doesn't happen—daily—for example, "I hope I don't get stuck in traffic." The pessimist's pattern is to consider the negatives and hope against them instead of anticipating the positives and working to bring them about.

Our theory:

- When it comes to physical appearance, a pessimist may be overly concerned that he or she might be judged negatively by others and so spends an inordinate amount of time in front of the mirror. An optimist is not overly concerned about appearance because he or she doesn't have to appear perfect to feel acceptable.
- On one item, there is a unique perspective. One of us, Jim Cathcart, feels that pessimists often hoard things for fear of missing a benefit, for example, saving papers for fear of missing something important. They tend to stack things for some future date when they will have the time and mood to deal with it. Optimists, according to Jim, tend not to collect things because they want to get the work done and out of the way to make room for whatever comes next. Optimists feel their next experience will be good.
- Pessimists tend to yield to temptation, feeling that they can't win over temptation in the long run anyway, so why try to be disciplined this one

time. Optimists, on the other hand, expect success, so they have less difficulty establishing good patterns with discipline.

In sum, pessimists get carried away by extra time spent on personal grooming, routines that distract from the relevant realities of life, and any activities that make them feel that they're delaying the inevitable disappointments in life. Optimists get on with life to make room for the next good thing.

Learned Optimism or Learned Pessimism: Your Choice(s)

Pessimists may indeed feel more anxious about social acceptance. They may feel more anxious about many things not going well, big and small. Psychologists have a term for such individuals when they suffer from this in the extreme—*neurotic*. We don't like that term because it connotes something very bad, when all it's meant to point out is that some people have a greater tendency to become anxious about smaller things than others. For example, some people tend to spend much more time on their work than they need to in order to ease their fear of being fired because they don't appear "perfect."

In the workplace, this tendency can come across as undue attention to details that are clearly irrelevant to bottom-line success. Sometimes it comes across as a control issue, particularly when foisted on underlings. For example, if the boss is a stickler for details that don't matter in most people's opinions, then it appears much effort is misplaced and subordinates feel frustrated about wasting their energy when more important things are being ignored.

In addition, the pessimist at work may find it difficult to use the Awareness Factor because he or she is so preoccupied with personal decision making that there's little energy left to listen to associates' points of view. Pessimists are more likely to rely on the Status Factor, insisting that things be done according to how they've been done in the past and not tinker with new ways of thinking. The optimist, on the other hand, is eager to hear others' viewpoints, expecting the best from associates' input. Here the Awareness Factor reigns supreme. The optimist at work doesn't worry about controlling trivialities that don't add to the bottom line. He or she looks at the long run and asks, "How much of a difference will this make next week, next month, next year?"

Optimism, appropriately experienced, can do wonders in the workplace. Expect success, and you're more likely to achieve it. Even when bad times come our way, as they inevitably do, the optimist will be less disheartened than the pessimist. For example, new salesmen at Met Life who scored high on a test of "learned optimism" sold 37 percent more life insurance in their first two years than their pessimistic counterparts. According to the author of *Learned Optimism*, Martin Seligman, optimism means seeing the world more accurately in terms of taking responsibility appropriately, neither denying nor overestimating one's personal fault when things go wrong.

So when things do go wrong, how do you go about assessing your own blame? What's your best approach? First, ask yourself, what needs to be done at this point to remedy what is left? If, for example, a customer or client has been harmed, what needs to be done to rectify the situation from this moment forward? Second, ask yourself what has been learned from this outcome that can help prevent similar mishaps in the future? And finally, ask yourself what will help for all to adjust to the situation as it is? Do not yield to the urge to give up and send up flares of distress. That would only spin the others in the organization into a frenzy of crises.

When I was a youngster working as a waiter at a summer camp, there was one weekend when many more parents and visitors came than had been expected. It seemed to my untrained mind that it would be impossible to even begin to serve so many people with only myself and two others as waiters. However, the owner of the camp astonished me. Instead of pulling out his hair, he dove into the kitchen, ordered the cooks to start preparing the food, and began serving the visitors himself, and then directed us to follow suit, dashing in and out of the kitchen with almost superhuman effort. Of course, after a few minutes of bedazzlement, the other waiters and I followed suit and began doing what at first looked impossible. It took just one individual who knew what he was doing to inspire the rest of us. The day was saved.

To my young mind, we should have anticipated the overflow of visitors and had more waitstaff. There was no point in even going through the motions of serving because we'd all look so foolish. The more realistic agility skills of the Performance Factor would reveal that there were hungry people, food for them to eat, and the possibility of getting the food out to them even if it took longer than everyone wanted.

ConnectAbility for Greater Accomplishments

Optimism can begin at the top—it certainly has the greatest capacity to influence from that position. The optimist sees what is and then adds to that what can be done to achieve the most, within the values of those in the organization, so that all feel involved in a creative enterprise.

Those who feel in charge of their lives, careers, and relationships have a high degree of ConnectAbility—just think of individuals like Donald Trump and Lee Iacocca. Those individuals who have confidence based on experience also have a sense of what they can accomplish and are able to attack challenges with gusto. Who would you want on your sales force, those with a high degree or low degree of ConnectAbility? Salespeople with highly perceived Awareness and Performance Factors can determine how high to aim, figure out what they have to do to reach those goals, and then muster the energy to achieve them. Those with a low degree of the Awareness Factor will be paralyzed by any challenge that they fear they might not accomplish, or at least be slow out of the starting gate. So

Tips for Advancing Your ConnectAbility

- **Expect to succeed** and, other things being equal, you're more likely to do so.
- **Expect—and enjoy—success** in the present rather than regretting past decisions or putting off enjoyment for the future.
- **Even when things seem impossible, take what action you can** and follow through to a successful conclusion.

how do you achieve a higher level of that special personality resource for yourself?

According to Albert Bandura, originator of the self-efficacy concept and social learning theory, the first step is to build your self-confidence in any challenging task by taking baby steps and making sure you succeed. Then gradually place the bar a bit higher, assuring you succeed before moving on to higher challenges. It's all in the coordination of challenge so that you ensure your success by staying one step ahead of failure.

The second mode, according to Bandura, is to find a mentor who already knows the ropes and in whom you feel sufficient trust to follow in his or her footsteps. Bandura calls this *modeling*. Just watch how it's done and do likewise, to put it simply. Also, it's good to have a supportive environment so you are reminded of your successes by those around you whom you deem important.

You may notice that all this involves being in the moment. Be in charge of your environment so that each moment is geared to be a successful outcome. You're not merely putting in the effort to enhance your future; you're actually succeeding in the moment to enhance your future. In modeling, you're doing what you see in the present and not rehearsing what you will do for the future. It's the Awareness Factor of success in the moment. It's not what you *should* be doing; it's what you *are* doing.

Learned Helplessness

The opposite of the Awareness Factor can be characterized as learned helplessness. That's what happens when an individual experiences a string of fail-

One (small) step at a time. When faced with overwhelming challenges at work, force yourself to take one small step at a time.

ures and takes from those experiences that he or she will never be able to succeed in similar circumstances. You've no doubt heard of how elephants are conditioned to being tethered to a small spike in the ground. The grown elephant could easily dislodge that small spike. But as a very young elephant, that spike was probably a large tree trunk and, try as it might, it could not budge it. So it learned to stop trying. With the passing years, the elephant grows larger and the spike becomes smaller, but the elephant has already learned that it is helpless to pull at the chain—the opposite of awareness of reality.

If we allow our own small failures to "teach" us not to resist, then we have learned not to try even though we have the resources to win if we should. After a certain number of failures, we may come to expect that we just don't have what it takes to make things work out in our favor.

Creating Success

Optimism in the workplace involves not only expecting positive outcomes but also explaining them in a manner coherent with such outcomes. Leading others with optimism means dealing with the chaos of uncertainty by formulating a successful expectation despite the uncertainty. Life is full of uncertainty and that's as true of the workplace as it is of any aspect of life. Optimistic leaders have a strong perceived sense of self-efficacy; they believe in their teams as well. Uncertainty for the pessimist can lead to "paralysis of analysis," so worried about the uncertain details that there is more fear than

Don't be held back by thinking small. Remember the big elephant tied down by a tiny stake—learned helplessness? You may have more power to overcome challenges than you give yourself credit for.

courage. The optimist, on the other hand, takes charge and "creates" success out of uncertainty.

Making work meaningful and enjoyable means being more comfortable in our own skins at work and relating at a level that is relevant to us. The worst-case scenario is hiding our true personalities to conform with what we think is expected of us and communicating at what feels like a very superficial level. So what can you do, as one single individual, to make your work experience more meaningful and enjoyable? Try being more open.

Dr. Jonathan Smythe considered the hypothesis that keeping our authentic self hidden is a drain on our energy—not only in terms of work productivity but also in terms of our general health. It's hard to be optimistic when you feel drained and listless. Optimism is generally characterized by energetic momentum, not lethargic passivity. Apparently, it takes a lot of energy to hide your authentic self.

So what are the benefits of being more open? Dr. Smythe recruited 465 patients suffering from either arthritis or asthma. Half the group was instructed to write 20 minutes a day, three times a week, about their daily activities in a framework of time management. The other half was instructed to write about "the most stressful experience they had ever undergone." The results of this study proved the benefits of openness. Those who wrote about the stressful experiences ended up substantially healthier. The arthritic patients writing about stress showed an overall 28 percent improvement while the other group showed no improvement. The asthmatic patients writing about their stressful experiences showed a 47 percent improvement rate as compared to a 24 percent improvement rate in those writing about less stressful, daily experiences. Sure, the "stress" group felt worse immediately after the writing experience, but over time they showed significant improvement in overall health. It's similar to having a bad tooth pulled—it hurts in the process but makes for healing in the long run. Maybe that's why it's hard to open up about deep pain—it is painful to do so in the moment, but it makes us much better overall. One conclusion from this research may be that keeping deep secrets of our painful experiences robs us of our health-maintaining energies and possibly of our potential for optimism.[1] In general,

Open up to someone. Find a friend to whom you can divulge your most stressful work challenges—a sure-fire way to reduce your stress and strengthen your resolve.

the more open we are about our deeper self, the healthier we are. It follows that there might be more meaning in our relationships for those who know us more deeply.

. . . Are the Luckiest People in the Workplace

One of my clients, a CEO of a clothing manufacturing company, always mentions his 10-year-old daughter during our consults. It's easy to see that he loves her deeply. He marvels at her musical ability; her humor; how her genuine, spunky smile charms people. It's easy to see how this love for his daughter keeps him in good spirits, helping him to smooth over the rough spots in his

Tips for Advancing Your ConnectAbility

- **Even if you need to take "baby steps" as you approach new challenges**, raising the bar with each success, the end result will be accomplishing your goal.
- **Avoid "learned helplessness"** by giving every challenge your best shot.
- **Reveal your authentic self** to those you trust by being more open about your emotions; you will end up becoming more self-confident and healthier.

daily responsibilities. By allowing his love for his daughter to stay active in his emotional awareness, he is more resilient to the challenges that come his way on a daily basis. For those without children, love of family, spouse, partner, or intimate friends could serve the same end.

Life is indeed precious and fragile. What we hold so dear to us is never guaranteed. The stories that make up the "Local" section of our newspapers are filled with personal tragedies—the loss of young people due to foolish traffic accidents, drug overdoses of those to whom celebrity has come at too early an age, sudden heart attacks of otherwise healthy men in the throes of a competitive game of tennis. A long life isn't guaranteed. Our loved ones are precious and the choice to acknowledge their place in our lives adds to the meaning of life.

When you consider that many of us spend more time with our co-workers than with our own family members, there is certainly a need to acknowledge those relationships, what they mean to us, and how to find joy in them on a daily basis. They do their best (most of the time) to interact with us so that our job is made easier. It's easy to take them for granted and to succumb to workplace competition that can influence our filters and take away from the spontaneity that comes from the joy of the moment. Acknowledging their value to us, in spoken words or written messages, lets them know they're appreciated and gives us the sense of satisfaction that our sincere appreciation does more to motivate them than material rewards.

How does one make a commitment to enjoying life? That is indeed a good question. The answer has much to do with how we "discipline" our awareness to focus on what we enjoy, whether that be in whom we choose as partners, both in life as well as at work; what we choose to do with our free time; what music we choose to listen to; which cultural pursuits we choose; and, most important, what degree of authenticity we choose as we relate to the world.

Here is a question worth considering: Is it possible that the more honest you can be about your authentic self with others, the more meaningful a persuader you can be? As you influence others in your sphere of leadership, whether you're CEO, officer, supervisor, manager, or team member, it still works the same way. Your authenticity, recognized by others, makes you a much more trustworthy individual, and therefore a much more effective persuader. Think of it—would you be more likely to put trust in someone who comes across as genuine or phony? Vulnerable or defensive? Open to your feelings or self-righteous? Those with a genuine personality, humanly vulnerable, and open to the feelings of those around them—with a high degree of the Awareness Factor— are in a much stronger position in terms of coming across with the power to persuade and influence.

Spirituality and Your Health

There is a great deal of research attesting to the findings that those who are connected with a house of worship or who have found some way of experiencing their spirituality are healthier and happier. There's something about identifying with a greater power, whether that be in church or in one's deeper values, that makes life more meaningful and fortifies one's sense of self-efficacy. You see, the ability to control one's world is now enhanced by that spiritual power. Yielding to a higher power, as we've heard so often, does wonders in terms of creating a sense of security and optimism.

Surely, we all know people who find meaning in material things, whether that means a bigger income, a more expensive and flashy car, or a conspicuous outfit. We've read in our newspapers about top-level executives—at Enron, WorldCom, AIG, and other companies that failed—to whom incredible incomes were more important than the welfare of their employees or integrity with their shareholders. Making millions seemed so important to them that they lied to the public and caused the downfall of extremely powerful organizations. It definitely begs the question: are these people truly *happy* in their own lives?

Material success is not necessarily an indication of inner happiness and meaning. And those with less to show in a material sense are not always the unfortunate on a spiritual or emotional basis. With an optimistic and meaningful outlook on life, we are less likely to judge ourselves on a superficial basis. Those who follow their inner values tend to be happier than those who are materialistic. They're also more likely to be seen as trustworthy and credible. That, of course, makes them more effective leaders as their ability to persuade others is enhanced. But being rich doesn't mean forsaking one's authenticity and humanistic values—simply consider Oprah Winfrey, one of the richest and most influential entertainment personalities of our time. To this day she has not lost her sense of values regarding authenticity and demonstrates a high degree of ConnectAbility.

Keeping Up (and Down) with the Joneses

Other than work and family, what is it we get out of social interaction? Why do we go to parties or get-togethers with no particular motive except to enjoy ourselves? What is it in particular that we enjoy or find meaningful about such social interactions? Maybe some of them are not so meaningful or enjoyable at times. Why is that? Psychologists have studied a concept called "social comparison theory." In downward comparisons, we compare ourselves with those doing less well than we're doing, and in upward comparisons we compare ourselves with those superior to us in some way or other.

Social interaction, particularly with those we first meet or see on rare occasions, gives us an opportunity to see how we're doing on a relative basis. If the difference is too great in a downward direction, we are likely to feel bored and uninvolved. If the difference is too great in an upward direction, we are likely to feel either inferior or that the other party is arrogant and self-centered. But if we are honest with ourselves and have a healthy Awareness Factor, we feel support for both parties, in both directions. We feel that we can enrich the lives of others, no matter what their status in life, should they be open to that.

Foolish Hope to Overcome Challenges

The pessimist sees the negative potential; the optimist sees the positive. In some cases, the optimist errs on the side of the positive, denying the negative aspects of dire circumstances. Think of it as the capacity for hope. In terms of

Tips for Advancing Your ConnectAbility

- **Show appreciation for those closest to you.** It's a challenge, but you won't regret doing so in the final analysis.
- **Show appreciation to your associates to become more persuasive**—a key element of leadership at any level.
- **Authentic values, as opposed to materialistic values, make for a greater openness to the meaningful aspects of life.** Don't overlook the treasures of appreciating the present moment.

evolution, those of our ancestors who had greater hope for survival, even in the most dire of circumstances, would be more likely to strive toward survival when the circumstances appeared impossible. The pessimists gave in early, but the optimists who denied the impossibility of the situation tried nonetheless. Some survived. They were able to pass on that genetic trait—call it "unwarranted optimism" or "foolish hope" or "denial strategy for self-preservation." Whatever you call it, it works.

Here's a very simple yet graphic depiction of what we're talking about. Imagine you're on a fishing trip. You catch a fish, remove the hook from its mouth, and place it on the deck. The fish has two choices: it can just lie there, accepting its fate, or it can continue to thrash around as it tries to get back in the water. If the fish accepts its fate, it's a goner, for sure. But if it continues to thrash around, not knowing what the thrashing might bring about, there's a small chance it will thrash its way over the edge of the boat and back into the water. That chance might be very small, but it's the only option available to save the day. Those fish that survive go on to pass their "unwarranted optimism" genes to the next generation of offspring. So foolish hope does spring eternal, in a genetic sense.

A series of studies by UCLA psychology professor Dr. Shelley Taylor looked at how some individuals actually improve their chances of survival even when given the terrible news of a mortal disease. Dr. Taylor has her own name for such unrealistic optimism—"positive illusions." Patients who chose to perceive their fatal diagnoses as smaller challenges than they really were did much better in terms of survival. It turns out that when individuals believe they have control over life's challenges, that sense of control gives them added motivation and energy to fight their disease. Dr. Taylor and her colleagues found that HIV-positive men who would not accept the fatal nature of their disease lived nine months longer than their counterparts who were more realistic.[2]

The bottom line is that whatever gives us a sense of control helps us to persist in overcoming challenging situations. In general, we do not advocate denial of reality, but when the reality is that we no longer have any control over life, then some positive illusion is in order. In other words, only in extreme circumstances, when all seems lost, is it advisable to bend the truth toward self-efficacy, toward the possibility that hope will overcome what others deem inevitable.

Recent research by Professor Daniel Gilbert of Harvard University has revealed that whatever happens to us, our brains choose to see the most rewarding meaning of events. Referred to as "the illusion of external agency," this process pushes us to attribute the rewarding outcome to some external agent, whether that be spiritual or human. We tend to settle on an understanding that is most satisfying, given whatever circumstances. According to Dr. Gilbert, the brain "tends to search for and hold onto the most rewarding view of events."[3]

Optimists Live Longer

In less dire circumstances, acceptance of reality is in order. In those situations there remains the possibility of control, and that's what keeps us strong, optimistic, transforming uncertainty into success. We get meaning from what we can control.

According to Martin Seligman, a pioneer of positive psychology, in an article published in *The Wall Street Journal*, "We don't know whether optimistic people are dumber or better than pessimistic people." But at least one economist believes that optimism, in moderation, is indeed advantageous. "A little bit of optimism," says Duke scholar David R. Robinson, in the same article, "is associated with a lot of positive economic choices." Optimists, Robinson and his colleagues discovered, smoke less, remarry more quickly when they do divorce, and save more. Others have found they are more likely to use sunscreen, take vitamins, and eat low-fat foods, thus living longer. But too much optimism, like drinking any wine, can be bad. Those who overindulge in optimism spend too much and don't plan past the following day.

Thinking as an Optimist

Dr. Seligman found in his research on learned optimism that there are three dimensions of an event that make us feel good or bad about our involvement: our degree of personal involvement, the degree of permanence we anticipate for a given event, and the degree and level of pervasiveness. So the next time you feel bad about an event that turns out poorly, look at how you explain it.

First, do you take personal responsibility for causing the negative outcome? Second, do you see the outcome as permanent and unchangeable, or is it something you can change if you put your energy behind it? Third, is this outcome going to affect your whole life, or can you put limits on its effects? If you see the outcome as your responsibility, unable to be changed, and affecting everything in your life, then you're thinking like a pessimist. On the other hand, if you can explain the event as having external causes (only part of which may be your responsibility), being easily changed if you marshal your resources effectively, with limited effect on the rest of your life, then you're thinking like an optimist.

So start thinking like an optimist. You're not totally responsible for everything. As a matter of fact, you're just one of many who make things happen at work. If you stay aware of your decision-making process, you're less likely to make foolish errors. It's human to err, occasionally. But by staying mind-

Is it really your fault? Check it out. It's unlikely you are *totally* responsible for a mess-up at work. Be realistic about that.

ful of your decisions and their consequences, you're less likely to make poor choices. Whatever happens is changeable if you focus on what exactly the worst part of the negative outcome is and put your energies toward rectifying it. Nothing is as pervasive as you are likely to imagine it if you can take an objective perspective.

A Lesson in Optimism

When I was just starting out in my career some years ago, after an all-day training program for professional speakers, I approached the main presenter to give her some feedback on her speaking style—constructive criticism that I thought would help her for her next presentation. I waited for a few others to end their after-talk chatting and then approached her. But instead of waiting for a comfortable moment after rapport had been established, I started right in with my feedback.

The speaker was overwhelmed in the most negative fashion you can imagine and became defensive. She retorted, "How do you know that? Did you check with others?" indicating clearly that she was offended. Here she was, after a day of presenting, at her most vulnerable moment, and I "attacked" her with what she saw as criticism, whether it was constructive or not. She was meeting with the officers of the organization next, and I could just imagine her outrage spilling over into their conversation as she billed me as the most insensitive dolt, destructive and pernicious. I myself was devastated. What was intended as helpful and supportive was received as aggressive and tactless. And now my standing in the organization (I was newly elected to the board) was tentative to say the least. I could just see myself being ostracized from the group I had hoped to become an integral part of. I could handle this situation as either a pessimist or an optimist.

Here's the pessimist version: I truly am an insensitive dolt. I took it upon myself to "attack" someone at her most vulnerable moment. How could I be so stupid! This event will change things forever. I'll never make my way back into the good graces of this group to which I aspired to be an integral part. This will affect my entire professional career. Every aspect of my career is tinged by this from now on and forever.

Here's the optimist version: I offered constructive criticism that no one else had the guts to offer. This feedback will make her good presentation even better in the future. She deserves to hear what will help her. I would want that if I were in her shoes. She took offense to it. Somehow she may not be as secure as I thought in terms of getting such feedback. I misjudged that aspect of her personality. Had I taken more time to develop a personal rapport with her, she definitely would have been more receptive and appreciative. I'm responsible for communicating effectively, though not responsible for her feelings. This is a lesson in the necessity for good rapport before giving potentially hurtful feedback. I won't forget that.

So, was I personally responsible? Absolutely, and so was the other party, making this a two-way proposition. Was the effect permanent and pervasive? Not at all, as I took charge of the situation to rectify the understanding of all those involved that my intent was benign. I took responsibility for my timing and pointed out what I learned about the importance of gaining rapport before offering constructive criticism.

I share this personal story to illustrate that this theory of optimism is only as good as its application to a down-to-earth, thorny problem.

Taking Responsibility

Is there a danger that the optimist overlooks the harsher aspects of reality in order to stay optimistic? Only under the most dire of circumstances, as we've seen. Otherwise, the optimist realizes what *is* and takes charge of a situation, giving it meaning as a controllable enterprise. Are optimists overwhelmed by unhappy circumstances that interfere with their rose-colored vision? Optimists are human and prone to being stressed by overwhelming misfortune but are less prone to such events than are pessimists.

Show your appreciation. Life is precious and fragile—live each moment fully and don't hide your appreciation for others.

If optimists explain unfortunate outcomes as not their personal responsibility, whom do they blame? According to University of Michigan psychologist Christopher Peterson, one of the originators of the concept of learned helplessness, most people look to themselves first. It's unlikely that any mindful person would totally extricate him- or herself from all responsibility. The optimist merely tries to be as objective as possible with ConnectAbility. If there's something to be learned from the personal aspect, so much the better, but there's more likelihood that the optimist will be more accurate about assigning personal blame.[4]

ConnectAbility means taking charge and fixing a situation to the greatest extent possible. In business it means seeing what *is* in terms of what can be done to remedy a situation, not resignation to failure. Optimism gives positive meaning to challenges by the control that can be manifested in changing things for the better. The dragon of pessimism can be slain—it just takes intention and commitment.

Tips for Advancing Your ConnectAbility

- **"Foolish hope" always trumps learned helplessness.** No matter how trying and difficult the circumstances, choose steps toward success.
- **Think moderately about extreme outcomes.** Whether an outcome is extremely good or extremely bad, remember that you're not the only cause of it, that even this won't last forever, and that it's not the center of the world.
- **No matter how challenging a situation, even those that seem impossible to control**, your best approach is to be realistic about the details, take charge, and aim for the best. That's all you can do and it's the best you can do.

Conclusion

CONNECTABILITY, AS WE can now see, is a complex interaction between you and the rest of the world, with a focus on business. Its main component, when the rubber hits the road, has to do with clarity of communication, particularly the aspect having to do with authenticity and awareness. Becoming a great communicator to build strong partnerships means delivering the message in a manner that influences as much as it persuades. That is to say that authenticity paves the way for a more subtle effect, where emotional honesty and a supportive attitude create a sense of trust. Defensive postures drop off and give way to clearer and deeper communication so that the job, whatever it is, gets done with more efficiency, as more information gets processed in a shorter time frame.

Business is best accomplished when individuals work together with a smoothly running team effort. The commercial aspect of business is best accomplished when influence to accept what is being offered is delivered with an authenticity that makes the prospect more open. In other words, what is seen as authentic has the greatest chance of acceptance.

Though this sounds simple enough, the devil, as they say, is in the details. No two situations are exactly alike, and so each one demands a unique perspective and a unique application of ConnectAbility. Business is always made up of people, so each of the eight keys of ConnectAbility has its particular use in any business interaction as it applies to the individuals at hand.

Share Your Power with Others

Sharing power by intelligent delegation—the right person for a particular responsibility—is key to effective leadership. Knowing individuals well is important. And the best way to bridge the emotional gap is to recognize basic needs for motivation and achievement. You'll do best when you're faced with a challenge that is attractive to you. The better a boss can get to know an employee, the more he or she has a sense of what challenges might inspire that person. What are your basic motives when it comes to recognizing the challenges that draw out your best talents? The very large framework of research on emotional intelligence has proven that we do much better at all aspects of business—from sales to management to production—when we can be more sensitive to the emotional dynamics of interpersonal communication.

Communicate with Authenticity

The research on neuroscience reveals that open communication is the best policy not only for mental health but also for more effective business. Stress damages the brain, when intense and extended over time, and sometimes in short duration if the stress is great enough. Good communication, particularly at an emotional level, soothes the brain but also, the research indicates, builds better processing networks *within* the brain. If we feel support in our work environment, then our brains can coordinate decision making more effectively by melding the rational with the emotional, logic with intuition. The best business decisions are made when logic and intuition work in tandem. Listening is key, of course, whether you aspire to become a better leader, salesperson, or some other position within your organization. It's all about ego, whether or not we can place our own aside while listening to others. And ego is not always easily managed.

Match Skills with Potential

Flow can be established by matching the challenge to the ability of the individual where that challenge is just enough without being too demanding. If it's too easy, the result will be boredom. If it's too hard, frustration can result. If you're the one making that decision, how do you discover the ability of an individual? By having that person open up and reveal inner aspirations and motivations and what successes have taken place in the recent past. A genuine interest in that person's welfare can communicate sufficient trust to share what really excites the individual in terms of challenge and potential for success. The Assessment for Managers and Supervisors at the end of this book can be of great help.

If you're managing others, then knowing them well is the key to success. Though self-awareness is not our main focus here, it's still essential, so that we can grow and maintain our own self-confidence. That confidence radiates to those we manage, encouraging them to trust us with their inner selves, vulnerabilities and all. That openness is what enables us to make the best matches between challenge and ability, between offering a product or service to a prospect and closing the sale, and between two associates.

Whatever we're attempting to communicate, it'll be easier if we minimize any perceived risk. The more open we can be about what we do know, the more successful our communication. Speak your truth clearly, show your support, and treat others fairly.

Express What Is Relevant and True for You

Honesty is not only a virtue, it's also a skill—a very complex one. What you share with whom and how is always the challenge. We all have the capacity for lying. We easily admit to little white lies and try to defend our egos against the accusation of bigger ones. We are highly prone to judgment from our friends—the worst outcome is social rejection.

How much of our inner selves and vulnerabilities dare we share, particularly in a competitive business environment? The answer has to do with a sensitivity to the context and relevance of any particular situation. A general disposition of authenticity and open support is always helpful. In general, women are more comfortable with such openness than men. As women grow their way into powerful positions in the business world, such openness may find greater receptivity.

We learn how to differentiate emotions in others from childhood experiences. As adults, we have already established habits of reading others. So ConnectAbility has much to offer us as we reexamine how to read faces, find our own inner "truths," and seek our own authentic messages. We all want to feel that we belong and are accepted by our peers, but at what cost? Connect-Ability reveals that deeper connections come with the risk of openness, when tempered by the values we've discussed.

Engage Your Audience with Humor

The saying "Laughter is the best medicine" has applicability to business as well. Daniel Goleman refers to a shared laugh as "empathic resonance . . . the shortest distance between two brains."

Another aspect of good communication is the ability to read faces accurately. Such skill clearly results in greater business success, especially sales. Research has shown that reading faces across racial lines is less accurate; diversity training helps to bridge that gap. And women, in general, are better at reading faces, except for the emotion of anger, to which men are more sensitive.

But reading faces is made easier for all by learning the basic components of emotions—fear, anger, and sadness being the unpleasant ones, and happiness being the pleasant one. That's really how a majority of social scientists see it, adding only two other emotions—surprise and disgust. To the extent we can learn to label these emotions, the more readily we can recognize them in facial expressions.

Recognizing our own emotions is important as well. It turns out the best decisions are made on the basis of both reason and emotion, or logic and intuition. So, to the extent that we can label our own feelings, we can then assign positive or negative values to tough decisions. The best business decisions come with the right combination of intellect, gut feelings, and a disposition of warm support. ConnectAbility aims at sharing appropriate emotions in a supportive and confident manner. Relevance of context and audience are of great importance. The proper expression of emotion in business communication is what leads to the greatest success.

Overcome Failure Through Acceptance

Accepting the reality handed to you is aided by the process of reframing negative events. Now that sounds like a paradox, doesn't it? So let's tackle it. Reality, as we hear, bites. Not everything that happens in the business world is pleasant and rewarding. Sometimes business outcomes hurt. But reframing helps us to accept whatever happens by looking for the silver lining and the lessons to be learned. All this is subsumed under the rubric of the agility skills component of the Performance Factor.

Coming from a position of mindful acceptance allows us to "take charge" of negative emotions and helps create a sense of control in overwhelming situations. This helps put us in a position of control and leadership at such times as we channel our rational mind to offer a model of sanity to those who are tempted to give in to dire circumstances.

Mindful acceptance is the discipline of taking a step back from emotional intensity and becoming more aware of what is happening in the moment. That helps us to accept whatever is happening without becoming too affected by it, when negative outcomes predominate. Being a great communicator in the face of such calm is a strong component of effective leadership.

Feelings are not to be relegated to the background. Richard Wiseman, author of *The Luck Factor*, believes that what makes people lucky is attending to their gut feelings. So we should not diminish our feelings but focus on them under normal circumstances, so we can become more aware of what "lucky" options surround us.

The best decisions are made with a blend of reason and gut feeling. Under dire circumstances, we don't want to be overwhelmed by feelings of fear, but otherwise we need to give our feelings equal attention. By acknowledging the fear and then witnessing it from some objective distance of mindful acceptance, we can begin to gain mastery over it. Our perception then becomes clearer. Greater awareness is enhanced by feelings of what is important in our work environment. The ordering of priorities is more easily accomplished by allowing our feelings to assist our rational decision making.

Maintain Awareness of Emotional Dynamics

The skill of labeling your emotions is a very practical one, giving you much more control over your emotional state. It also makes you a better communicator because you're able to be clear about your message.

Conflict is largely due to a lack of clear communication. Once the deeper motivations of two opposing parties are uncovered, a possible resolution is made much easier. And these deeper motivations are characterized by emotion as much as rational fact. In the absence of clear communication, threat feelings predominate and cloud good judgment. So, both for communication style as well as content, emotional clarity is of the essence.

Becoming a great communicator while building strong partnerships means mastering the complexity of emotions, in self-awareness as well as in speaking or writing. Emotional awareness is a key component of ConnectAbility. If we're clear about our emotional signals, then there will be less confusion in our message. And that's where authenticity comes into play.

To bring it all together, here are the four steps of emotional awareness:

1. Bring Awareness of Influence into play by acknowledging your basic communication style (including the predominant emotion affecting you) and how you're coming across to others.
2. Bring Awareness of Context into play by focusing on what's needed in the existing business context and the Desired Outcome.
3. Bring your agility skills into play by considering the most productive options and the ones for which you feel most comfortable taking per-

sonal responsibility, while delegating other aspects most effectively, if possible.

4. Make your decisions based on serving others as well as your own needs, for lasting results.

Challenge Yourself by Taking Charge

There are two ways of dealing with challenge—that of the optimist and that of the pessimist. By and large, pessimists tend to react with anxiety to events that optimists would consider trivial. Optimists tend to save their anxiety for the bigger issues. Optimists, almost by definition, expect success more often than their counterparts. And we know that expecting success breeds success, just as expecting failure leads to that as well. In times of severe stress, the pessimist is beaten down before beginning to respond. The optimist acts quickly and decisively and fosters a "can-do" attitude that just might save the day—and often does.

So how do you become an optimist in your own field of business endeavor? Simply by taking on small challenges at first, succeeding at them, and then raising the bar bit by bit. The habit of success soon replaces learned pessimism and you're on your way to thinking like a winner.

How ConnectAbility Skills Can Make You More Successful

Decision making is best accomplished using your ConnectAbility skills before the meeting. If possible, discuss your new vision with your close associates to create a base of support for the success of this vision when final decisions are made. The more radical your vision is, the more it differs from the status quo, the greater the need for agreement from your base of support. As Jack Welch puts it, "change happens faster and deeper in organizations when people are emotionally engaged."

It's our strong belief that the most successful meetings—that involve change or new visions—are merely the dessert of the meal. Appetizers are the feelers put out to see who might be in agreement and who might not. The main course is the hard work of authentically sharing, listening, and compromising. The dessert—the formal meeting itself—is the culmination of the work leading to the agreement.

The Performance Factor offers the fastest route to critical change. Some meetings don't offer the opportunity for prior discussions and processing. In those cases all, or most of, the work must be done at the meeting itself. That might occur, for example, at board meetings, the members of which are quite busy and who have not yet developed close-enough relationships with the other member to allow for prior processing. What works best for us when we head such meetings is to listen carefully enough to differing viewpoints so that we can then summarize the essence of each point of view to the speaker's satisfaction. Then, at the point of closure, we do our best to authentically integrate what we've heard so that no speaker of any viewpoint feels dismissed. Finally, we articulate the conclusion that is true to our initial intent, but now integrating the meaty and substantial portions of what has been shared.

When garnering support from your base, project the listening-skills component of the Performance Factor by demonstrating that you're not only listening but, more important, hearing what others are saying. Acquire the skill of summarizing the substance of each person's contribution at the end of each meeting, before adding your own vision, integrating it into the context of what you've heard. The presentation-skills component of the Performance Factor involves combining the hearing and presenting in such a manner that all in the present group feel heard, appreciated, and then inspired by the new vision of which they can now feel a part.

Appreciate the overriding principle of business behavior—people act on the basis of their own interests—and you won't be surprised. The Awareness Factor involves full acceptance of the others' perspective, without idealizing their motives as altruistic or necessarily benign. Always offer others the benefit of the doubt until and unless you're forced to do otherwise. Keep refining your use of the Performance Factor, without sacrificing your authenticity, to adjust to each individual's unique challenges. When others begin to admire your diplomatic manner, you'll know you're moving in the right direction, particularly when your adversaries are offering that compliment with sincerity.

One part of the definition of politics is "scheming and maneuvering." That sounds very undermining. When you can make your agenda acceptable to your adversaries without being seen as political, then you've most likely succeeded in making others feel accepted and appreciated not by politics but rather by your ability to really and deeply appreciate your adversary with authenticity.

Merely appearing authentic just won't work. You communicate not only by what you say and how you say it but also by the impression you make overall, and that includes your physical appearance, not only in choice of fashion and style but also in terms of facial expression and demeanor. Naturally, an authentic smile is much more convincing than a "forced" smile. Charisma is not only the powerful message communicated through words; it's also the convincing emotion in face and body posture.

The conundrum remains how to "appear" authentic. The solution is to *be* authentic. Learn how to transcend differences and to appreciate the person beyond the posturing and defensiveness. No one is born bad, evil, or unlovable. The more you can understand and appreciate the context of the other's perspective and how it was arrived at, the stronger you can accept and appreciate that individual at an authentic level. And that's the authenticity in your own demeanor that will contribute to your charisma.

Although we seem most comfortable with simple answers, the real answers are never that simple. Your authentic approach can allow you to appreciate the complexity of most challenges. The greater your understanding of the context-awareness component of the Awareness Factor, the more you appreciate that most challenges are not easily understood as simplistic good vs. bad thinking. It's hardly ever a matter of one person being completely right and the other being completely wrong. More realistic is the awareness that there are different perspectives of the same matter, based on different experiences leading up to the issue or conflict. It's always easy and tempting to simplify matters geared to our own perspective and to build a fortress of defensive thinking around them. That only builds the sense of conflict and frustration over the long run. Better to invest energy up front in bridging the gap between factional issues and then to resolve them more easily over time with more give and appreciation for the need to negotiate with a sense of authenticity.

Putting It All Together

The bottom line of ConnectAbility is authenticity; all aspects of becoming a great communicator and building strong partnerships are affected by this factor. Whom would you trust more readily, someone with an authentic personality or someone dictating demands with hidden motivation? Authenticity can be acquired by applying the eight keys of ConnectAbility to all aspects of business relationships; however, like all critical skills, this takes discipline and time.

Becoming a great communicator while building strong partnerships begins with an awareness of your own emotional self, as well as the needs of others, often hidden behind well-learned defenses. This involves staying aware of how you affect others in terms of bringing out their potential when you address their deeper needs. It also involves a keen appreciation of the organizational values and who, among your associates, are key to serving those needs with a sincere sense of contribution.

So where to start? First decide which of the eight keys you find most appealing and start with that one. Try it on for size and see what modifications you can make in your current communication style as it relates to that key. Go through each key at your own pace, and then start again with another key, but each time with a bit more focus and intention. Get a companion—an associate at work or a personal friend, or even your significant other—and get some feedback. How does your emerging ConnectAbility come across? What differences do you yourself notice? Eventually you may want to choose one key and spend a month focusing on its benefits.

The ability to connect with others is always our most magnificent challenge. Yet ConnectAbility, with its focus on awareness, presentation skills, and the ability to influence the right individuals for the desired business outcome, is the best approach for becoming a great communicator and building strong partnerships, both at work and within our own personal lives.

Greater success at creating the most productive relationships, whether in achieving your own career goals, managing others, or in sales, is yours to achieve. Just remember to take one step at a time, and you'll soon find yourself well on your way to mastering all eight keys of ConnectAbility.

Appendix

THIS SECTION CONTAINS two self-scoring assessments: The first is designed to test the ConnectAbility skills of individuals and help them to learn the most about themselves and advance their level of ConnectAbility. The second will help managers and supervisors interview their direct reports when either hiring or evaluating someone for annual review or promotion. For best results when taking both assessments, stay honest.

ConnectAbility Test for Individuals

Assign a number to each statement as it applies to you, according to the following scale:

5 Always
4 Usually
3 Sometimes
2 Rarely
1 Never

_____ 1. I prefer to keep others in line so that they do not overreach their assignments.

_____ 2. I maintain a veneer of professional objectivity.

_____ 3. I assign responsibility for failures to others.

_____ 4. I avoid trying to influence or persuade others.

_____ 5. I react to every problem with a show of anger.

_____ 6. I avoid confronting discrepancies, trusting they'll disappear with time.

_____ 7. I avoid emotional reaction to other's feelings.

_____ 8. I express my angry feelings.

_____ 9. I keep my personal philosophy apart from my business personality.

_____ 10. I display my feelings openly.

_____ 11. I prefer generalizations to specific details.

_____ 12. I maintain my focus on global issues, allowing others to take care of the details.

_____ 13. I avoid problems, hoping time will cure them.

_____ 14. I delegate high-priority problems.

_____ 15. I make sure to keep my feelings separate from any public statements.

_____ 16. I "keep my cards close to the vest."

_____ 17. I listen to what others have to say.

_____ 18. I focus on others' feelings.

_____ 19. I judge others on the basis of their past performance.

_____ 20. I take care not to be overly influenced by others' feelings.

_____ 21. I desire to do good for others.

_____ 22. Intellectual integrity interferes with my sense of authority.

_____ 23. I am confident in my own abilities.

_____ 24. I encourage others to greater levels of risk taking.

_____ 25. I am addicted to executive power.

_____ 26. I am open with others about my own personal philosophy.

_____ 27. Inner calm means more to me than spontaneous expressiveness.

_____ 28. I enjoy my ability to influence and persuade others.

_____ 29. Conflicts and problems are dealt with early.

_____ 30. I have an open eye for discrepancies and attend to them early.

_____ 31. I keep negative emotions at bay in any crisis.

_____ 32. I am challenging without being abrasive.

_____ 33. I offer support whenever I can, both in public and in private.

_____ 34. I express angry and forceful feelings in moderation.

_____ 35. I am sensitive to personal boundaries.

_____ 36. I make others feel as if they are unique contributors.

_____ 37. I stay uninvolved and impersonal.

_____ 38. I share my personal feelings and opinions.

_____ 39. I am open and forthright in all situations.

_____ 40. I allow others to lead without supervising them.

_____ 41. I bring different factions together, even if they're opposed.

_____ 42. I am open to opposing ideas.

_____ 43. I focus on relevant details of problems.

_____ 44. I take personal responsibility for unfavorable outcomes.

_____ 45. I am candid with staff members about controversial findings.

_____ 46. I make exceptions to policy to acquire important information.

_____ 47. I delegate high-priority problems whenever I can.

_____ 48. I am open to others' feelings, even in the heat of argument.

_____ 49. I give priority to the feelings leading up to a conflict.

_____ 50. I stay sensitive to the effect of expressing my own feelings.

_____ 51. Spontaneous feelings are warmly and heartily expressed by me.

_____ 52. I am able to obtain support and assistance easily.

_____ 53. I communicate my intentions clearly.

_____ 54. I am honest about my own feelings and intentions.

_____ 55. I focus on others' feelings and intentions.

_____ 56. I help others understand themselves.

_____ 57. I encourage others to exceed job expectations.

_____ 58. I enjoy complex challenges, and obtain satisfaction in sorting out the facts to clarify the solution.

_____ 59. I enjoy complex challenges and find my work personally fulfilling.

_____ 60. I'm just as aware of my human vulnerability as I am of my personal power.

Scoring

To score this test, compare your answers to the answer key below. Assign 5 to each matching response, 4 to any response that is one removed from the correct response, 3 to a response that is 2 removed, and so on. For example, if the correct response is 3 and you chose 3, then assign yourself 5 points for that item; if the correct response is 3 and you chose 2, then assign yourself 4 points; if the correct response is 3 and you chose 1, then assign yourself 3 points. In other words, for each item, your score is 5 points minus the deviation from the correct response (5 – deviation). If 1 is the correct answer and you answered 3 (a deviation of 2), then your score for that item is: 5 – (the deviation of 2) = 3. Then add up all assigned scores.

Answer Key

1. *Never (1)*. The high ConnectAbility individual doesn't keep others in line. Instead, she empowers and encourages others to reach for the best they can be.

2. *Sometimes (3)*. The high ConnectAbility individual fosters no deceit or preference and is emotionally forthright, yet is governed by a clear sense of propriety. The individual with ConnectAbility expresses enthusiasm and excitement through the ranks and, when called for, can show occasional feelings of anger. Yet all this is counterbalanced by inner calm.

3. *Never (1)*. The high ConnectAbility individual does not refuse or deny responsibility.

4. *Never (1)*. One goal of ConnectAbility is to influence others.

5. *Rarely (2)*. The high ConnectAbility individual is frank, forthright, and candid, occasionally revealing feelings of anger and frustration.

6. *Never (1)*. The high ConnectAbility individual is always open to resolving conflict as soon as possible, to form clarity out of chaos, sometimes

even expressing feelings of anger and frustration, but only when appropriate and only in moderation.

7. *Sometimes (3).* Because of the high ConnectAbility individual's perceptiveness, expressive personality, and helpful attitude, he or she is certainly going to react to others' feelings, but maintains a durable, consistent center against undermining efforts such as gossip and manipulative favor seeking.

8. *Rarely (2).* Occasional expression of forceful, angry feelings has a place in the personality of the high ConnectAbility individual.

9. *Rarely (2).* The high ConnectAbility individual is authentic and genuine, saying what is meant, offering support through nonverbal means, and finding the leadership role personally meaningful.

10. *Usually (4).* The high ConnectAbility individual is authentic and free of pretense, expressing genuine, true feelings spontaneously, tempered with sensitivity as to effect.

11. *Rarely (2).* The high ConnectAbility individual often gets involved with relevant, specific details in order to clarify complex problems, as well as to resolve conflict.

12. *Rarely (2).* Dealing with specific details helps uncover the truth.

13. *Never (1).* Time, by itself, usually cures problems, but hardly ever in time to satisfy the high ConnectAbility individual, who acts quickly to resolve conflict, sometimes putting off regularly scheduled meetings when urgency requires it, taking initiative to confront discrepancies even before others become aware of them.

14. *Rarely (2).* The high ConnectAbility individual hardly ever delegates high-priority problems or procrastinates in dealing with them.

15. *Rarely (2).* See item 9.

16. *Rarely (2).* The high ConnectAbility individual is authentic, frank, and forthright, candid in the face of crisis, and pulses with vibrant personality. He encourages others through enthusiasm and zeal. However, when confronting discrepancies, he starts off with a gentle, warm approach.

17. *Always (5).* This is the essence of ConnectAbility.

18. *Always (5).* Same as item 17, only more so.

19. *Sometimes (3).* Bringing out the best in others means accepting them on the basis of what they offer rather than what idle gossip says. On

the other hand, past performance, accurately documented, cannot be
ignored.

20. *Always (5).* Sensitivity to others' feelings is crucial to the high Connect-
    Ability individual, but, when resolving conflict, she takes care to be
    open to both sides. She also avoids being overly influenced by manipu-
    lative favor seeking or malicious gossip.

21. *Always (5).* The high ConnectAbility individual assists others in growing
    to understand themselves, and offers a model for open communication.
    He also is generally supportive through nonverbal means, aiming for
    mutual respect and propriety, even in the face of deceit and evasiveness.
    Candor in the face of crisis indicates trust and respect for the adminis-
    tration as a whole.

22. *Never (1).* Intellectual "integrity" does not prevent the high Connect-
    Ability individual from expressing angry feelings in moderation when
    that is called for. A vigorous, spirited personality allows for an effective
    sense of authority without sacrificing intellectual integrity.

23. *Always (5).* The high ConnectAbility individual enjoys the abilities to
    influence and persuade others, impressing others with the ability to
    make things happen, and feels competent in accomplishing most chal-
    lenges. Above all, this individual is confident and self-assured.

24. *Always (5).* By being warmly expressive and intensely involved in help-
    ing others, the high ConnectAbility individual encourages others to
    greater levels of risk taking and achievement.

25. *Never (1).* The high ConnectAbility individual is not addicted to execu-
    tive power, but finds deep fulfillment in personal relationships.

26. *Usually (4).* Openness about personal philosophy helps others know the
    direction of the high ConnectAbility individual and makes for better
    communication across the board.

27. *Always (5).* An inner calm helps the executive to be more sensitive to
    others' feelings. Although typically expressive, warm, and candid, the
    high ConnectAbility individual approaches areas of potential conflict
    with calmness and counterbalances an outgoing personality with an
    inner calm. The extroverted personality has an underlying inner self-
    assurance.

28. *Always (5).* An effective leader, the high ConnectAbility individual always enjoys the challenge of persuasion.

29. *Always (5).* Even before others become fully aware of them, the high ConnectAbility individual senses trouble spots—poor performance problems, conflict, low morale—and takes the initiative in resolving such problems.

30. *Always (5).* See item 29.

31. *Always (5).* Although capable of demonstrating angry feelings when necessary as a last resort, the high ConnectAbility individual initially aims for mutual respect and propriety with a gentle, warm approach.

32. *Usually (4).* A receptive ear can calm those who are upset and helps deliver clarity out of chaos. The high ConnectAbility individual invites parties of a conflict to paint their respective scenarios as early in the conflict as possible and offers the benefit of doubt as much as possible, resorting to anger only when that is the only remaining alternative.

33. *Always (5).* The high ConnectAbility individual makes people feel special and unique through nonverbal as well as verbal means.

34. *Rarely (2).* See item 32.

35. *Always (5).* In this time of sensitivity to issues of sexual harassment, there is no room for any lack of sensitivity to personal boundaries.

36. *Always (5).* See item 33.

37. *Rarely (2).* The high ConnectAbility individual gets involved with others, making them feel special, identifying with their feelings, sharing his own feelings, and having an open ear to anyone who can shed light on existing problems. He is enthusiastic and supportive yet is quick to approach any area of possible conflict, being confronting when necessary, and enjoys getting involved in helping others.

38. *Usually (4).* See item 10.

39. *Usually (4).* See item 10.

40. *Rarely (2).* High ConnectAbility individuals stay close to staff members, encouraging them to greater self-understanding and personal growth, dealing directly with problems that fall under their levels of responsibility.

41. *Always (5)*. The high ConnectAbility individual brings differing factions together to focus directly on the challenges at hand, arriving at clarity in the face of chaos.

42. *Always (5)*. The high ConnectAbility individual is always open to hearing both sides of any conflict, willing to make exceptions to policy in special cases, and attends quickly to discrepancies, approaching them with warmth and sensitivity. This individual is open to all feelings from the gut.

43. *Always (5)*. The high ConnectAbility individual gives priority to the facts leading up to a conflict and looks for relevant, specific details.

44. *Always (5)*. The high ConnectAbility individual gets directly involved as problems arise and takes personal responsibility for unfavorable outcomes.

45. *Always (5)*. As soon as possible, after coming up with a resolution to a problem, the high ConnectAbility individual makes new findings known to all staff members in as candid and honest a manner as possible.

46. *Usually (4)*. The high ConnectAbility individual is willing to make exceptions to policy to facilitate the discovery of important information that might contribute to the resolution of a problem.

47. *Rarely (2)*. See item 14.

48. *Usually (4)*. See item 17. This is where the rubber hits the road in managing with ConnectAbility. Even in the face of conflict, the high ConnectAbility individual gives priority to understanding the facts and feelings leading up to the conflict. Uncovering deceit is accomplished by a gentle, perceptive approach, until there is no alternative except to fight intransigence with the vigor of an angry response.

49. *Always (5)*. See item 48.

50. *Always (5)*. Although openly expressive, the high ConnectAbility individual is nonetheless sensitive to the effects of such openness, governed by a clear sense of propriety.

51. *Usually (4)*. See items 10, 38, and 39.

52. *Always (5)*. By being very clear about intentions, the high ConnectAbility individual can obtain the support and assistance necessary to reach corporate goals.

53. *Always (5).* See item 52.
54. *Always (5).* See item 52.
55. *Always (5).* See item 17.
56. *Usually (4).* With the wisdom of experience, the high ConnectAbility individual helps others to understand themselves, but not in a manner that comes across as pushy.
57. *Always (5).* By making others feel special and bringing out the best in them, the high ConnectAbility individual encourages others to exceed job expectations. This is enhanced by making thoughtful pairings between individuals and their challenges.
58. *Always (5).* With the ability to bring different factions together to focus directly on complex problems, the high ConnectAbility individual can probe the facts and emerge with elegant solutions, in large part due to the ability to listen carefully and deeply to all voices.
59. *Always (5).* Dealing with conflicts quickly and courageously, the high ConnectAbility individual experiences work as personally fulfilling and satisfying.
60. *Always (5).* Keenly aware of the human condition, the high Connect-Ability individual counterbalances a sense of personal power with a sense of humility.

240+ points	**Superstar.** You're in a position to be a great support to those around you.
180–239 points	**Star.** With a bit of extra effort you can really get ahead.
120–179 points	**No prize yet.** But at least you're honest—that's a great start.
60–119 points	**Nowhere to go but up.** You've got a great future ahead of you if you apply yourself.

ConnectAbility Assessment for Managers and Supervisors

This survey outline will help managers and supervisors interview their direct reports when either hiring or evaluating someone for annual review or promotion.

1. Awareness of Context: Knowing the overall perspective and identifying appropriate support

- Knows concerns about forthcoming problems, real or imagined.
- Has strong preferences, accurate gut reactions.
- Is optimistic and excited about role in organization.
- Is able to make the best of a situation by taking into account existing feelings and how to best make use of them.
- Monitors one's feelings to anticipate where things are heading and what others need.

Question: Tell me about a time when you had a deep gut feeling about something that would help at work and you decided to go ahead and explore that possibility and how you figured out whom the right person would be to talk with.

Evaluation: Did the individual have a clear sense of his or her feelings about something of benefit to the organization? Was there optimism and excitement about this initiative? Or was there indifference about inner feelings, particularly about feelings where things might be heading at work?

- − − Unaware of preferences or inclinations. Indecisive. Complains frequently about others not being cooperative.
- 0 Fairly easygoing. Easily influenced by others but may complain about unfavorable outcomes.
- + + Clear and decisive, yet open to new information. Always takes responsibility for outcomes. Able to understand others' motivations.

Comments: _____

_____

_____

2. Personal Differences: Nonjudgmental attitude—bringing out the best in others

- Accepts each individual on the basis of what he or she offers at the present moment, not on what others may think happened in the past.
- Fosters an attitude of concern and support.
- First meeting characterized by openness to potential of the new relationship.

Question: Tell me about a time when you first met someone in the workplace who was later important in your life and how you first reacted to that individual. Can you remember how you felt about this person? Concerned? Respectful? Cynical? Guarded?

Evaluation: Did the individual use words reflecting courtesy and respect or negative judgment? Was there openness to positive potential or a guarded cynicism? Did the individual express support at this first meeting or put up a defensive façade?

- − − Self-righteous, all blame falls on others, fearful and suspicious.
- 0 Little or no consideration for the feelings of others. Somewhat aware of the feelings of others.
- + + Makes others feel special. Encourages them to reach for the best they can be.

Comments: _____

_____

_____

3. Personal Differences: Perceptiveness—helping others to understand themselves

- Effective in communicating one's perceptiveness.
- Understands others and uses this to help them understand themselves.
- Makes others feel appreciated.
- Identifies with others' feelings.
- Exhibits sincere intention to help others.

Question: How often do people at your organization come to you for advice? Tell me about a situation in which you remember helping someone going through a rough time, sitting down and explaining to him or her what part that person played in the predicament.

Evaluation: Do others come to the individual often or rarely? When they do, is there a meaningful exchange of self-understanding or just superficial advice?

- − − Totally unaware of others' feelings.
- 0 Occasionally listens to what others express emotionally.
- + + Perceives others' feelings very clearly and helps them understand themselves.

Comments: _____

_____

_____

4. **Presentation Skills: Optimistic Mental Attitude—fostering genuine optimism**

- Authentic, frank, and forthright about one's intentions.
- Articulates goals clearly and precisely.
- Expresses optimistic feelings warmly.
- Easily obtains support for future goals.

Question: Where do you see yourself five years from now? Ten years? How do you feel about your role in the organization?

Evaluation: Is individual specific and candid about the future goals, or vague and inappropriately optimistic? Is there a sense of spontaneous engagement of feelings and excitement about future possibilities at the organization, or merely pat answers with no feeling expressed?

- − − Words bear no relationship to feeling. Negative about future.
- 0 May be genuine on occasion but doesn't always say what is really meant. Neutral toward future.
- + + Deeply genuine and spontaneous in expression of true feelings of optimism for future.

Comments: _____

_____

_____

5. Agility Skills: Presence—taking personal responsibility

- Shows openness to facts and feelings as they exist at the moment.
- Has open attitude, even to those who may be upset.
- Makes direct contact with those with whom he or she is in conflict.
- Doesn't procrastinate in dealing with problems.
- Is open to all perspectives.

Question: Could you tell me about a time when you were involved in a difference of opinion with someone at work and how you dealt with it?

Evaluation: Does the individual express habits of being open to facts as others see them, or is there an attitude of avoidance? Is there a commitment to taking responsibility for one's actions, or is it always the other's fault?

   – – Avoids problems at all costs.

   0 Solves problems from a cautious distance.

   + + Has an attitude of "the buck stops here."

Comments: _____

_____

_____

6. Awareness of Context: Relevance—supporting the truth

- When confronted with problem, digs into details without fear.
- Gets others to focus on relevant details.
- Explores pertinent facts as they relate to germane issues.
- Is open to suitable suggestions.
- Can separate fact from fiction.

Question: Could you tell me about a situation when two people had different versions of something? And could you focus on how the real truth was uncovered?

Evaluation: Does the individual reveal a desire to get to the core of the truth, or does the person finesse things so that he or she comes out looking good? Did the initiative to uncover the truth come from the candidate or from the other party?

- − − Hides behind abstract generalizations.
- 0 Makes no effort to focus on relevant facts.
- + + Demands specifics supporting the truth.

Comments: _____

_____

_____

7. Presentation Skills: Expressiveness—creating smooth communication

- Shows sensitivity to issues of individual or group.
- Is open and forthright according to a particular audience.
- Makes others at the organization feel accepted and involved.
- Forges strong sense of group identity by supporting and inspiring others.
- Encourages others to higher levels of dedication to the organization.

Question: Can you tell me about a time when you were put in charge of a group and the first time you got to address the group? (If no group responsibility, change "group" to "individual.") What did you talk about and how did it go?

Evaluation: Does individual focus on others' feelings? On the relevance of issues given the circumstances of the moment? On the need to inspire others? Were candidate's own feelings shared appropriately? Or were candidate's feelings totally ignored?

- − − Impersonal and uninvolved, not letting others know where one stands.
- 0 Sometimes personable but not specific about how one feels.
- + + Candid about personal feelings when relevant and appropriate.

Comments: _____

_____

_____

8. Awareness of Others: Supportiveness—fostering loyalty and a sense of contribution to the organization

- Is personable and supportive.
- Has warm voice, facial expressions, eye contact.
- Shares personal feelings and opinions.
- Is extremely sensitive to personal boundaries.
- Makes others feel as if they're making significant contributions.

Question: Tell me about a time when you were supporting someone in their career path—maybe coaching or mentoring, or just managing—and this person depended on you for your support. Tell me the best you were able to do and how you did it.

Evaluation: Is this individual able to focus on the dynamics of support and understanding? As the story is told, are there hints of warmth on the face and in the voice? Is such warmth demonstrated throughout the interview? Did the candidate take advantage of the employee in any way because of the power relationship?

− − Impersonal and uninvolved. No consideration for others' feelings.

0 Shows some concern and support for others.

+ + Compassionate and understanding, clearly expressed.

Comments: _____

_____

_____

9. Agility Skills: Boldness—resolving conflicts early

- Takes initiative in confronting discrepancies.
- Is able to keep negative emotions at bay by approaching with a warm, gentle attitude.
- Offers benefit of doubt with support.
- Has ability to be candidly challenging without being abrasive.
- Perseveres in pursuit of honesty, matching emotional strength with others.

Question: Can you tell me about a time when you were put in a position to resolve a conflict between others? How did you approach it? How were you brought into the situation in the first place? What did you do when things got emotionally intense?

Evaluation: Did the individual provide the initiative to first get involved in this conflict resolution? How fair-minded yet candidly challenging was the individual? Are there indications that the individual was able to stand up to others who got intense without "losing it"? Or is conflict resolution something the individual has managed to avoid totally?

- − − Avoids discrepancies until they become unavoidable.
- 0 Approaches conflict, but with intense feelings.
- + + Approaches conflict early and with warmth and openness to hearing all facts.

Comments: _____

_____

_____

10. Expectations—offering a model for effective leadership based on clear expectations

- Finds managing others meaningful and fulfilling.
- Can see things from different points of view and encourages others to have open minds.
- Enjoys resolving problems and conflicts.
- Is excellent at time management.
- Takes satisfaction in concrete results.

Question: What was your greatest challenge in managing others? Specifically, could you tell me about a time you had to resolve a problem with little time to spare and what you enjoyed most about the outcome?

Evaluation: Was the individual able to manage things within a given time frame? Able to see the other's point of view? Most important, does the individual express enthusiasm at the prospect of using one's personal power to overcome management challenges?

- − − Feels ineffectual and is cautiously guarded.
- 0 Feels competent in accomplishing most challenges.
- + + Finds leading others deeply fulfilling. Sense of personal power balanced by sense of humility. Inner serenity about sense of personal responsibility.

Comments: _____

_____

_____

11. Awareness of Influence: Self-Assurance—encouraging others to greater achievement based on their own ideals

- Enjoys helping others.
- Possesses self-assurance that makes others feel calm and assured about their own roles.
- Encourages others to dig deep into their own personal resources.
- Is able to influence and persuade others with eloquence.
- Maintains inner integrity.

Question: I'd like to know how others feel about you. How would your worst enemy describe you? (After candidate's answer, then:) How about your best friend?

Evaluation: Is the individual able to talk openly about shortcomings without embarrassment? Do strengths include helping others, particularly when they are distressed? Does best friend's account include assurance and encouragement by the candidate?

- – Expressionless, hiding anxieties and insecurities.
- 0 Communicates effectively about feelings when prodded.
- + + Highly self-expressive and self-confident, admitting to some shortcomings.

Comments: _____

_____

_____

12. Agility Skills: Communicating effectively at leadership and sales

- Quick to take on the challenge of leadership.
- Decides and acts quickly.
- Is able to motivate others to rise to the challenge.
- Takes responsibility for one's decisions.
- Can delegate with courtesy and respect.

Question: Do you remember a time when you were thrust into a problem of leadership without much preparation? What happened and how did you get along with the others?

Evaluation: How quickly was the individual able to persuade others to accept his or her leadership role? Was delegation characterized by courtesy and respect? Did the individual feel comfortable with newly acquired power?

- − − Always defers to others when it comes to making decisions. Avoids responsibilities.
- 0 Can take on leadership responsibilities when forced to do so, but reluctantly.
- + + Conveys a sense of leadership in an authentic manner.

Comments: _____

_____

_____

13. Presentation Skills: Determination—getting results quickly and effectively

■ Is a determined, self-directed hard worker.
■ Works hard, even under the worst of circumstances.
■ Is highly assertive and can even be aggressive when appropriate.
■ Is bottom-line oriented.

Question: Do you remember a time when you were forced to make decisions more quickly than ever and get others to work with you, even though you had to be real tough to get them going? Were you ever put in such a position?

Evaluation: Is individual focused enough to push ahead alone and strong enough to coerce uncooperative others to join up? Is there sufficient drive to get the job done despite setbacks? Or has candidate avoided such challenges both by avoidance and because others realized his or her lack of drive and determination?

− − Laid back and withdrawn. Takes path of least resistance. Always accommodating. Tries to please everyone.
0 Can get results when others help with focusing. Sometimes gets easily sidetracked.
+ + Uses time highly productively. Clear focus on bottom line. Can work alone or get others to join in when necessary.

Comments: _____
_____
_____

14. Listening Skills—able to make others feel heard

- ■ Is reliable, dependable, and loyal.
- ■ Is very considerate of others' needs.
- ■ Gives much thought before taking action.
- ■ Is not overly dependent on public recognition.
- ■ Is people-oriented, both socially and work-wise.

Question: Have you ever been in a position to get someone to open up when he or she wasn't that relaxed? What's the best way to get someone like that to open up? What's your experience with that?

Evaluation: Does individual show indications of thoughtful consideration of others' needs? Of sincere caring for others and respect for the mutuality of self-disclosure? Or is the feeling process closed down?

- – – Self-centered and self-involved. Has very difficult time understanding others' points of view. Very closed about sharing feelings (own and others').
- 0 Can understand others' points of view, but only reluctantly. Can talk about feelings, but reluctantly.
- + + Finds it easy to get people to open up. Shares warm feelings and common experiences easily. Open, straightforward, and sincere.

Comments: _____

_____

_____

15. Awareness of Influence: Frustration Control—being aware of and expressing anger constructively

- Becomes aware of frustration before it gets emotional.
- Can label it at that point.
- Removes self from frustration, either physically or psychologically.
- Figures out how to express it constructively.
- Takes steps to create logically productive outlet.

Question: Do you remember your greatest frustrations? Can you recall one of those and tell me how soon you realized the situation was becoming frustrating and how you dealt with it?

Evaluation: Does individual show an awareness of signs of impending frustration by labeling such feelings in advance? Is there awareness of how to detach from such frustrating events while logically productive outlets are devised? Or does candidate allow frustrations to build up to destructive levels?

- – – Unaware of sources of frustration. Allows emotion to build beyond control.
- 0 Takes out frustration on others, damaging existing relationships.
- + + Always aware of potentially frustrating situations and detaches long enough to figure out productive way of dealing with it.

Comments: _____
_____
_____

16. Agility Skills: Self-Efficacy—dealing with the stress of change

- Is consciously aware of need for change to meet ongoing challenges.
- Labels feelings in reaction to the stress.
- Deals with theoretical worst-case scenario.
- Identifies specific change needed for particular challenge.
- Explains specific strategies needed for best coping reaction.

Question: What about stress? Can you recall one of your most stressful times and how you dealt with that?

Evaluation: Was individual able to label feelings of concern before stress became full-blown? Was he or she able to return to calm while figuring out specific strategies to cope with that particular challenge? Or was there a helpless, pessimistic attitude?

- − − Doomsayer. Takes worst-case scenario as inevitable and feels helpless.
- 0 Makes necessary changes, but not very effectively and fears unsuccessful outcome.
- + + Able to stay calm while analyzing worst possible outcome and marshals resources to return to satisfactory conditions while remaining optimistic.

Comments: _____

_____

_____

17. Awareness of Influence: Stress Management

- ▓ Is usually relaxed whatever the degree of surrounding stress.
- ▓ Lives healthy lifestyle, including nutrition and fitness.
- ▓ Is self-aware of feelings on an ongoing basis.
- ▓ Can label intense feelings of anxiety or anger without getting caught up in them.
- ▓ Can manage relaxed feelings once intense feelings are recognized, in part by taking positive action, in part by trusting the resources that are available.

Question: Can you share with me your best coping mechanisms for dealing with stress? How did you deal with stress the last time you remember it being an issue?

Evaluation: Does individual mention anything about lifestyle of good nutrition and fitness? Can individual label feelings of early upset before they become problematic? Can individual take positive action, taking advantage of support from ongoing network?

- − − Easily overcome by anxiety and stress. Unable to monitor these feelings until they're taken over and become unmanageable. Indecisive. Pessimistic.
- 0 Not given to succumbing to stress except for exceptional cases, then becoming less productive.
- + + Chooses healthy lifestyle. Aware of incipient, uncomfortable feelings. Nurtures dependable and trustworthy resources by dependable networking. Does not personalize "disasters."

Comments: _____

_____

_____

18. Awareness of Influence: Self-Esteem—nurturing good feelings about self

- Is open-minded about self-image, not rigid.
- Has at least one individual with whom total openness is a habit.
- Is an active member of at least one highly supportive group, either personal or professional.

Question: How would you describe your strengths and weaknesses? Whom do you talk to about such things?

Evaluation: Is individual able to discuss strengths and weaknesses with equal candor? Is the overall feeling about self realistically positive? Are there people with whom individual can share support and confidentiality? Are most relationships comfortable and supportive? Or does individual feel lonely and marginal, projecting an image of carelessness and defiance?

- – – Feels inner sense of insecurity, marginal—not belonging. Finds it difficult to accept compliments. Does not take pride in personal appearance.
- 0 Good sense of self most of the time but given to periods of self-doubt whenever things aren't going right.
- + + Enthusiastic about role in life—both personal and work. When with others, feels comfortable opening up. Comfortable with own shortcomings.

Comments: _____

_____

_____

19. Awareness of Context: Work Ethic—finishing what is started

- Enjoys work at the organization.
- Is inner-directed and self-motivated.
- Enjoys the challenge of overcoming difficulties.
- Takes pride in achieving "the impossible."
- Takes pride in high-level performance.

Question: What accomplishments are you most proud of? Tell me about overcoming a great challenge that left you feeling very proud and one that you failed at. Tell me about the failure experience first, then the success.

Evaluation: Does individual demonstrate a pride in overcoming difficulties, in continuing to build personal and job-related skills, in setting goals with precision? Or is candidate lazy about deadlines, sloppy about important details, and easily distracted?

− − Lazy. Habitually misses deadlines. Sloppy about important details. Easily distracted, particularly by social interruptions.

0 Gets things done on time when there is clear structure but may fall short otherwise. Works better under supervision than without.

+ + Strong sense of purpose. Takes pride in accomplishment, especially under difficult circumstances, and delivers quality work on time. Looks for clarity of detail in goal setting. Enjoys building new skills and sharpening existing ones.

Comments: _____

_____

_____

Scoring

Each item is scored on a 5-point scale, from minus 2 to plus 2. Final scores determine the following:

−38 to −10	Reject
−9 to +9	**Ready for ConnectAbility training**
+10 to +38	**Good model for training**

Notes

Introduction

1. **Australian study:** Research by Christie Napa Scollon of Texas Christian University cited in Rodgers, J.E. (2006). Altered ego. *Psychology Today*, Dec., p. 75. Study of more aware executives earning higher profits: Stein, S.J., Papadogiannis, P., Yip, J.A., & Sitarenios, G. (2009). Emotional intelligence of leaders: A profile of top executives. *Leadership and Organization Development Journal, 30(1)*, 87–101.

Chapter 1

1. **Sanofi-Aventis study:** Jennings, S. & Palmer, B.R. (2007). Enhancing sales performance through emotional intelligence development. *Organizations and People, 14(2)*, 55–61. **Increased sales:** Insurance agents—Hay/McBer Research and Innovation Group, 1997. L'Oreal findings—Spencer, L.M., Jr. & Spencer, S. (1993). *Competence at Work*. New York: Wiley & Sons. Recent evidence linking emotional awareness with superior sales skills can be found in Rozell, E.J., Pettijohn, C.E. & Parker, S.R. (2006). Emotional intelligence and dispositional affectivity

as predictors of performance in salespeople. *Journal of Marketing Theory and Practice, 14(2)*, 113–124.

2. **Lower turnover:** Hay/McBer study—Spencer, L.M., McClelland, D.C. & Kelner, S. (1997). *Competency Assessment Methods*, Boston: Hay/McBer. Furniture retailer—Hay/McBer Research and Innovation Group, 1997. Beverage firm—McLelland, D.C. (1999). Identifying competencies with behavioral-event interviews. *Psychological Science, 9(5)*, 331–339.

   Merit increases: Greater merit increases research is by Lopes, P.N., Grewal, D., Kadis, J., Gall, M. and Salovey, P. (2006). Evidence that emotional intelligence is related to job performance and affect and attitudes at work. *Psychothema, 18*, 132–138. Research linking job satisfaction with high emotional intelligence from: Kafetsios, K. & Zampetakis, L.A. (2008). Emotional intelligence and job satisfaction. *Personality and Individual Differences, 44(3)*, 710–720.

3. **Management skills:** The study on emotional expressivity by Groves, K.S. (2006). The effect of leader emotional expressivity on visionary leadership, leadership effectiveness and organizational change. *Leadership and Organizational Development Journal, 27(1)*, 556–583. Study proving the ability to teach leadership skills is from Groves, K.S., McEnrue, M.P. & Shen, W. (2008). Developing and measuring the emotional intelligence of leaders. *Journal of Management Development, 27(2)*, 225–250. Research on "high-powered" managers having greater emotional intelligence from: Dries, N. & Pepermans, R. (2007). Using emotional intelligence to identify high potential. *Leadership and Organizational Development Journal, 28(8)*, 749–770.

   Job success: "Agreeableness" affecting salary and adaptability affecting perceived job success from: Rode, J.C., Mooney, C.H., Arthaud-Day, M.L., Near, J.P. & Baldwin, T.T. (2008). Ability and personality predictors of salary, perceived job success, and perceived career success in the initial career stage. *International Journal of Selection and Assessment, 16(3)*, 292–300. Self-awareness and success—Boyatzis, R.E. (1982). *The Competent Manager*. New York: John Wiley & Sons. Air Force study—GAO report, Military Recruiting, submitted to Congress on Jan. 30, 1998. Top-level executives from 15 global companies—Spencer, L.M., Jr., McClelland,

D.C. & Kelner, S. (1997). *Competency Assessment Methods*, Boston: Hay/McBer. Evidence of team leaders influencing their team members from: Koman, E.S., Wolff, S.B. (2008). Emotional intelligence competencies in the team and team leader. *Journal of Management Development, 27(1)*, 55–75.

4. At Ford, the "outside" is optimistic. *The Wall Street Journal*, July 23, 2007, B2, and from Naughton, K. (2008) Where survival is job one. *Newsweek*, Dec. 15, p. 9.

5. Ramos, R.T. (2008). Home Depot earnings top expectations. *Atlanta Journal-Constitution*, May 21, C1–2; Bond, P. (2007). Home Depot boss takes page from founders' book. *Atlanta Journal-Constitution*, Feb. 25, F1–F8. The Home Depot annual meeting was held at the Galleria in Atlanta on May 22, 2008, where CEO Blake bravely took questions and "gripes" from shareholders. Blake's reaction to hard economic times from Ramos, R.T. (2009). Home Depot CEO gives up bonus. *Atlanta Journal-Constitution*, March 31, A7.

Chapter 2

1. Williams, K. (2005). *Love My Rifle More Than You*. New York: Norton. Incident and quotes taken from chapter titled "At the Monastery," 108–121, from public presentation by Ms. Williams at DeKalb County Library in Decatur, Georgia.

2. Sanfey, A.G., Rilling, J.K., Aronson, J.A., Nystrom, L.E. & Cohen, J.D. (2003). The neural basis of economic decision making in the ultimate game. *Science, 300*, 1755–1757.

Chapter 3

1. Levinson, W., et al. (1997). Physician-patient communication. *Journal of the American Medical Association, 277*, 553–559.

2. Camerer, C.F., Loewenstein, G. & Prelec, D. (2004). Neuroeconomics. *Scandinavian Journal of Economics, 106(3)*, 555–579; Camerer, C.F.

(2003). Strategizing in the brain. *Science, 300(5626),* June 13, 1673–1675. Also see Camerer, C.F. (2003). *Behavioral Game Theory.* Princeton, NJ: Princeton University Press.

Chapter 4

1. Material about Catalyst from Hymowitz, C. (2005). In the lead. *Wall Street Journal,* Oct. 24, B1.
2. Peterson, D. (2006). *Jane Goodall: The Woman Who Redefined Man.* New York: Houghton Mifflin; Goodall, J. (2005). *Harvest for Hope.* New York: Warner Books; Goodall, J. (1999). *Reason for Hope.* New York: Warner Books.
3. Zac, P., Borja, K., Kurzban, R. & Matzner, W. (2004). The neurobiology of trust. Program 203.23 presented at the 34th annual meeting of the Society for Neuroscience, San Francisco, California, October 23–27.
4. Description of BDOs can be found in Bradshaw, J. (2008). Behavioral detectives patrol airports. *The National Psychologist, 17(4),* July/August, 10. No Lie MRI and Cephos are described in Kluger, J. & Masters, C. (2006). How to spot a liar. *Time, 168(9),* Aug. 28, 46–48.

Chapter 5

1. Research cited in Elfenbein, H.A. & Ambady, N. (2002). On the universality and cultural specificity of emotion recognition. *Psychological Bulletin, 128,* 203–235. Research by K. Kawakami cited in Jan. 17, 2009, issue of *The Economist, 390(8614),* 77–78.

Chapter 6

1. Tabibnia, G., Craske, M., & Lieberman, M. (2005). Linguistic processing helps attenuate physiological reactivity to aversive photographs after

repeated exposure. Poster presented at the 35th annual meeting of the Society for Neuroscience, Washington, D.C., Nov. 12–16.

2. Beauregard, M. (2005). Scientists unravel brain circuits involved in joy and sadness. News release from Society for Neuroscience, Aug. 6.

Chapter 7

1. Russell, J.A. & Barchard, K.A. (2002). Toward a shared language of emotion and emotional intelligence. In L.F. Barrett & P. Salovey (eds.), *The Wisdom in Feeling* (363–382). New York: Guilford.

Chapter 8

1. Smyth, J.N., True, N. & Souto, J. (2001). Effects of writing about traumatic experiences. *Journal of Social and Clinical Psychology, 20,* 161–172.

2. Taylor, S.E., et al. (2000). Psychological resources, positive illusions, and health. *American Psychologist, 55,* 99–109.

3. This research was described in Begley, A. (2005). Science journal. *Wall Street Journal*, Oct. 28, B1.

4. Peterson, C., et al. (1998). Catastrophizing and untimely death. *Psychological Science, 9,* 127.

Index

About the Authors

DAVID RYBACK IS an internationally recognized authority on emotional and social intelligence in the workplace. A respected consultant and speaker across the United States, Europe, and Asia, he remains at the forefront of the latest research on applications of emotional awareness and related aspects of business communication and leadership.

He is an active member of the National Speakers Association, with board membership experience, as well as an active member of the Atlanta Press Club. He has been a columnist for *Business to Business*, an associate editor of a national psychology journal, and a member of the editorial board of *Georgia Psychologist*. He has been a columnist for *Speaker*, the magazine of the National Speakers Association, with a distribution of over 5,000 to the most influential speakers across the globe.

Ryback is the author of over 60 professional articles and innumerable book reviews in such publications as *Psychology Today*, the *Atlanta Journal-Constitution*, *Creative Loafing*, *AHP Perspective*, and *Business to Business*, among others. He is also the coauthor of *Psychology of Champions* (Praeger, 2008) and author of *Putting Emotional Intelligence to Work* (Butterworth-Heinemann, 1998).

He has been a professor at the University of Maryland (Overseas Division) and Emory University's School of Business. A former corporate consultant with Rohrer, Hibler & Replogle in Montreal, he has also done research and published on such topics as perception affected by mind-set, emotional intelligence, interpersonal communication, scholastic achievement, and enlightened management.

After publishing his book on emotional intelligence, Ryback founded his consulting and speaking business, EQ Associates International (www.eqassociates.com). In response to the demand for his speaking and consulting services, he has traveled across the country and to Europe, the Mideast, and the Far East, where he speaks and consults. He can be reached at David@EQassociates.com or 404-377-3588.

JIM CATHCART IS a former president of the National Speakers Association and recipient of its highest awards, including the Cavett Award, the prestigious Golden Gavel, and the CPAE Speaker Hall of Fame Award. In addition to his heavy involvement in public speaking, he is a top trainer, executive consultant, and president of Cathcart Institute. For more than 30 years he has been an influence on hundreds of thousands of people worldwide in ways that grow their business and expand their lives, addressing such major corporations as John Deere, Precision Tune, BMW, and others.

DAVID NOUR IS a featured speaker for corporate, association, and academic forums and one of the foremost thought leaders on the quantifiable value of business relationships. His company, The Nour Group, solves Fortune 500 client challenges with intracompany as well as externally focused Strategic Relationship Planning—the process of transforming valuable business relationships into execution, performance, and results.